Pockets of Change
Stories of hope for a world transformed

Published by:
Hungry For Life International
45950 Alexander Avenue
Chilliwack, BC V2P 1L5
Phone: +1 (604) 703-0223
www.hungryforlife.org
www.pocketsofchange.org

Editor: Kristine Den Boon
Layout & design: Justin Keitch
Cover design: Justin Keitch

ISBN: 978-0-9917696-0-5 (sc)

Printed in the United States of America

Cover Photo: Orphans Rachel and Adam
share a drink from a water tap at Noah's Ark
Children's Home in Mukono, Uganda. See
From nobody to somebody on page 64 to
read about Noah's Ark.

Foreword

A world transformed starts with one life transformed. One life transformed leads to a transformed family, church, community and eventually a country. The stories between these covers are only a few samples of the lives that have been impacted through our work of facilitating partnerships. Over the past decade, Hungry For Life has had the incredible gift of serving churches and groups in Canada and the US, helping them help churches and groups in many developing countries.

Hungry For Life is committed to addressing spiritual and physical poverty. It is our spiritual and moral poverty in the West that significantly contributes to the physical poverty in developing countries. We have found that when we go and spend ourselves on behalf of those who are physically suffering, we encounter the presence of God and our lives are changed. Every short-term team that goes out to serve comes back saying that the materially poor have far more to give us than we have to give them.

When we talk about poverty and a world transformed, we are conditioned to think about people in developing countries who are trapped in physical poverty and extreme suffering. We have images in our minds of starving children, depressed communities and hopeless situations. We are led to be believe that the only way we can do something about the brokenness of the world is to give money. We only ever hear the bad news. You won't find that in this book.

This book is full of good news. It is full of stories of change. Change on both sides of the world. It was produced to motivate you with hope and not with need. It was produced to draw attention on the great things that the Church is doing around the world. Most of all, it was produced to shine the spotlight on Jesus and His Kingdom.

Dave Blundell

Executive Director,
Hungry For Life International

Acknowledgements

This project wouldn't have happened without a committed team of people helping us along the way. From vision to completion, these individuals are to thank for the book you're now holding.

Above all, we wish to thank our Saviour, Christ Jesus. He made us who we are, He blessed us in a way that allowed us to do this project and to Him we give all the honour and praise. To God be the glory, great things He has done.

Thank you to Hungry For Life (HFL), for allowing us to work with you and letting us glimpse the powerful, life-changing work you are doing:

To Dave, who gave us an opportunity to work with HFL, provided us with the concept for this project and who believed in us and encouraged us.

To all the HFL staff, for the incredible, God-honouring, selfless work you do. This team is full of compassion, grace and love, and we have been humbled as we worked with this amazing group.

To Corrina, for always keeping us on track. You were our constant point person at HFL, chaired dozens of meetings and were with us from start to finish and every moment in between. Most importantly, you never gave up on us as the months turned to years.

To Ryan, for your vision, collaboration on the logo design, creative feedback and for helping us the whole way through from the first meeting to the final product.

To Jeremy, for allowing us to share our journey through the use of a clean, easy-to-navigate website and for your technical expertise throughout the whole project.

To Angela, Ginnie and the rest of the TPS crew, for all the work setting up detailed itineraries, booking flights, arranging accommodations, tracking budgets and the million other details that allowed us to travel smoothly and simply.

To the project managers, for sharing your expertise, for allowing us to see first-hand the work that goes on with HFL's project partners, for giving of your time in helping prepare us and for answering many questions while working on the book.

To Chad, for imparting your rich and varied knowledge about the different cultures we would be immersed in, helping us prepare for travel and giving us an idea of what we were getting into.

To Ginnie, for your help with the index. Your thoughtful process and thoroughness helped create a very user-friendly feature of the book.

To Steve, Diane, Mary and Gerry—the team leaders we had the privilege of spending time with on the field—for allowing us to join in with your teams while still helping us stay on track with POC. You guided us through cultural differences, integrated us into the group and cared for and encouraged us.

We are so thankful for the team that supported POC:

To all those who supported us financially and in prayer, we are truly thankful. Your donations covered travel expenses and allowed us to make this book a reality. Thank you for trusting in us and our abilities, and covering us with prayer as we traveled great distances and went through many challenges.

To those who housed and hosted us on home soil, thanks for your warm hospitality and willingness to share your space with us, including the Toyotas, the Davies, Mark Prins, the Penners, the Hannigans and the Argues. A special thanks to Butch, who stored all our worldly possessions. Your kindness allowed us to save money and gave us peace of mind that our tea kettle was never very far away.

To Justin, for your support and generosity in loaning us your wide-angle lens. Your action allowed some of the best photos in this book to be captured.

To Dr. Cherniwchan, for giving Justin yellow fever. But seriously, thank you for all the vaccinations to help us stay healthy as we traveled to very diverse climates with many different health risks.

To our copyeditors—Kathy, Shirley, Michelle and Elke—who carefully read through each story, checked spelling and helped turn a jumble of words into readable stories.

To our book editor Kristine, for your expertise on the publishing world, for your meticulous attention to grammar, for a final read-through of all the stories and for honest critique as we worked to narrow down the final story selections.

To Mike and Kathy, for all your support, especially countless hours of baby-sitting while we put the book together.

Thank you to the people whose stories and photos fill the pages of this book:

POC wouldn't have happened without the support of HFL's project partners. These people are doing incredible work for God's glory and allowed us to see and hear about it. They shared their passion with us so we could share it with you.

We were privileged to spend time with some amazing teams on the field. Thank you to Southside, Coquitlam Alliance, Hillside and the Chilliwack Mennonite community, for allowing us to piggyback on your trips. Without seeing teams in action, we wouldn't have had a clear picture of how missions affects change. Thanks for new friendships and shared experiences.

We interviewed more than 250 people and took over 26,000 photos. Thanks to each person we connected with through our lens and notebook. We wish we could share every story because they are all worth hearing. Thanks for being real and honest, for being personal and for trusting us with your story. Without the willingness of individuals to let us be intrusive with our questions and camera, there would be no book.

By using specific stories of the spiritual and physical transformation of people and communities, we desire to motivate individuals to be a part of a movement of compassion and justice, realizing their potential to effect global change.

Annabel

She was one in a sea of faces at Noah's Ark Children's Home in Mukono, Uganda. But in my mind, she stood out like she was the only one there.

Annabel. The name is sweet, innocent. It is a child's name but it belongs to a young girl with a very tragic history. While at Noah's Ark we followed her as she played on the swings and in the grass, ourselves full of disbelief that such a happy child could have such an awful story.

Annabel was born in October 2006. In July of 2008, she was found abandoned in a garbage container. A woman found her and told police she would take care of the child. Three months later, she too decided she didn't want Annabel anymore and left her with the police. Noah's Ark welcomed her in as they do all their abandoned children— with open arms and loving hearts.

She had been abandoned by not one but two different families. Staff at this Christian-based nonprofit organization knew it would take time for her to trust again given her obvious fear of abandonment.

But as a resident of Noah's Ark, Annabel has become a lively, energetic girl. She has a smile that can light up a room and the ability to hold you captive with her pinkie finger.

Annabel: a young girl with a tragic past. →

We spent just a short time with Annabel, but it had an impact on both of us. Before we left Noah's Ark, we had a chance to pray for Annabel. We prayed she would grow up to be a strong Christian woman, grounded in her faith. We prayed she would be protected and would trust her Heavenly Father, who never abandons His children.

It was a powerful moment for us, to realize we held a child in our arms that was left for dead in a garbage can and was now a beautiful three-year old girl full of life and so much love.

This little girl could grow up to be the change that Uganda needs. Maybe she will lead her people by a faithful example. Maybe she will become a doctor who will help mothers to not die during childbirth. Maybe she will simply grow up, and that alone will be an example to parents who want to abandon their kids. The point is, she has those options now thanks to Noah's Ark, an organization that is saving kids like Annabel.

Justin plays with Annabel in the yard. ↘

Huanca Huanca

← pronounced: Wonka Wonka

The blind receive sight, the lame walk, those who have leprosy are cured, the deaf hear, the dead are raised, and the good news is preached to the poor.
LUKE 7:22b

It's only 90 kilometres from the central city of Cusco yet it takes four hours to reach on a bumpy dirt road cut from the steep Peruvian mountains. Psychologically, Huanca Huanca might as well be 900 kilometres away from anywhere.

Huanca Huanca is not much but a cluster of approximately 120 Cusco-Quechua families living in simple homes on the hills surrounding the central school grounds. However, this isn't the quaint farming community you might picture. This is a spiritually dark place.

Oppressive.

Sexual abuse is prevalent and considered almost normal, even expected. The history of violence here stretches far, with parents doing to their children what was done to them by their parents. Alcohol abuse is rampant. Men lie drunk outside their dark dirt homes at 10 in the morning. To pay for work, alcohol is a common currency. And with that vice comes all the associated issues: violence against women, poor diets and broken families.

Physical health here is dismal. Residents are unable to farm or buy food with enough nutrients for their bodies. They are also uneducated in dental and sanitary cleanliness. Water is not clean. With a lack of education, the people of Huanca Huanca have been unable to come up with solutions to better their way of life. They're trapped in a cycle of poverty and pain.

"There was fornication, adultery—everything here," shares Anselmas, a community leader in Huanca Huanca.

Yet there is hope. In a community just coping, the tide is turning. Like in Biblical times, the eyes of the blind have been opened, the poor have heard and are turning to the Truth.

When asked how the Gospel first came to Huanca Huanca, Anselmas tells an interesting story. There was a man, a dangerous thief who would assault people as they walked the road between his village and Cusco.

But then the thief heard of Christ, became a Christian and started to evangelize to the people he used to terrorize, including in the community of Huanca Huanca.

But then the thief heard of Christ, became a Christian and started to evangelize to people he used to terrorize.

Anselmas
and his wife
Justina.

Huanca Huanca is nestled in the mountains, miles from anywhere.

"Now we have reconciliation and forgiveness in God," declares Anselmas.

Some became Christians during that time. In this oral society, people were unable to read the Bible and it became a matter of the blind leading the blind. With a lack of understanding of what it means to be a Christ-follower, many fell away and went back to their old lifestyles.

"We were doing the best we could in giving people the Gospel to the best of our knowledge. But people were leaving the church," Anselmas remembers.

Then a few years ago, a group called ATEK showed up in Huanca Huanca. This Christian organization, based out of Cusco, is dedicated to training Quechua people, focusing on empowering the church and its ability to impact the local community.

Knowledge was limited here. One of the issues residents faced before ATEK came was the language barrier in reading their own Bible. Students are taught to read in Spanish even though their native tongue is Quechua. ATEK is teaching people how to read their own language so they can not only read the words but comprehend them as well. It's opening up the entire Bible to the people here and enabling them to study the Word and learn how it applies to their lives.

ATEK is providing marriage counselling to help strengthen families. Couples are learning how to listen to each other, how to love each other and how to treat each other. In a male-dominated society, men are learning how to love their wives as Christ loves the Church. They also have children's ministries, leadership training, community development programs and audio-visual programs to bring the message of Christ to more people through tools such as the Jesus film and an audio Bible.

Now people are coming back to the church and even non-believers are changing because of the example of Christians around them. Anselmas and his wife Justina are very pleased with what has been happening in their tiny town through the power of the Gospel.

"It is going well now here with the help of ATEK," Anselmas states. "We've learned how to walk with God and to live our lives for God."

Justina says the children especially have benefitted from this community transformation. They're seeing healthy relationships with their parents, and the children are better behaved as a result. They're becoming Christians and witnessing to their teachers. The children now want to go to other communities to witness too.

"I pray that there'd be a generation of kids that will be living within the will of God, and will be able to grow and to use what they know of Christ and to live their lives within His will," says Justina. "We've seen real change in the kids."

Through ATEK, short-term missions teams have started coming to Huanca Huanca too. ATEK partnered with a church in Stony Plain, Alberta. Beach Corner Evangelical Free Church is committed to staying involved for the long haul. This church has really connected to the community of Huanca Huanca. In a few short years, they have seen God work through them to reach the lost here.

In terms of physical aid, Beach Corner has committed to paying for an agricultural expert to work within the community. That program is already reaping rewards, with a test patch harvested and community members interested in learning more. Through better farming practices, the people will get the nutrition they need to survive.

Anselmas says every time the team from Beach Corner comes, there is an impact in the community.

"It makes us proud, to see Christians from so far away worshiping the same God we do," says Anselmas. "They came with an attitude ready to serve, to be open. We admired them for that."

Pastor Bill Meier, senior pastor at Beach Corner, commented on the team's visit to Huanca Huanca during their 2009 mission trip.

"The people were encouraged by our visit," he said. "There is great potential for the children and youth of Huanca Huanca, and there was a great response to the services that were held."

Pastor Bill shares the story of one man telling the team, "Before you came I thought Christianity was for the poor people and the illiterate." Then he saw the sacrifice the team members made to spend their money and time just to come visit them in their village and realized Christianity was for everyone.

Yet through this relationship, the people of Huanca Huanca aren't the only ones being impacted. Beach Corner team members talk about what they've seen and taken away from their time in Huanca Huanca too.

"It affected [team members] in various ways. For a few, it was so overwhelming they were in survival mode for the whole time. But for others, it confirmed a real heart for

missions," says Youth Pastor Bryan Meier, Pastor Bill's son. "The trip unified the vision we [as a church] had. The vision fits so perfectly."

For Taylor Stobbe, who was 17 when he went on his church's missions trip, it was an experience he won't soon forget.

"It's a cliché because everybody says it, but I really grew a lot from being there," he says.

There is still a long ways to go in Huanca Huanca. The church does not have a building, and would like to find their own space to construct a permanent structure. There are less than 100 adults out of more than 240 residents attending the church, with 38 baptized members so far. And one of their largest concerns is the lack of a pastor. Without a trained leader, there is a fear the church could backslide again, or go in a wrong direction because of a lack of guidance. ATEK is also working to train up pastors,

and at some point the congregation would like to have one of their own be trained for church leadership.

But things are definitely looking up in Huanca Huanca. There are dozens more stories just like this one playing out across the mountainous territory of the Cusco-Quechua people through ATEK's work. Anselmas prays the revival will continue, and that the church here will grow and mature in Christ.

"We want to see a revival and explosion of the Gospel throughout the whole community," he concludes.

They came with an attitude ready to serve.

John & Nadia

John and Nadia are a living story of a selfless couple who sacrifice in every aspect of their lives. They give above and beyond what is possible. And then they give some more.

They help those who everyone else has forgotten. Like Pasha, an invalid paralyzed from the chest down. The whole world abandoned Pasha, immobile in a bed in a house in a splotch on the map known as Shishkino, Ukraine.

Shishkino is more a memory of a place than a place. If the tiny village fell off the edge of the world tomorrow, likely no one would notice it was gone. The people here live depressed and depressing lives. And here Pasha lays, day in, day out, night after night. Monotony of an existence in a country with little assistance for the crippled.

Pasha wasn't always this way. As a teenager, he got his driver's license, drove drunk, hit a tree and trashed his spine.

More than 10 years ago, Pastor John began leading Bible studies in Shishkino to reach out to the people here. Pasha's sisters began attending the study and both gave their lives to God. Their home ended up burning down, and the very first short-term missions team that came from Canada to help John and Nadia's ministry bought a place to serve the dual purpose of a home for the sisters and a house church for the small group of believers in Shishkino.

When Pasha became handicapped, the sisters opened their home to take care of their brother.

Pasha's room bears a single lightbulb above his bed, a dirty striped carpet below. White walls with teal accents. His two sisters care for him, themselves so fragile they have a hard time coping.

The sisters look after the building with the same care that they devote to Pasha. On Sundays, he listens to the singing and sermons from his bed.

Nadia was instrumental in getting Pasha into a rehabilitation centre recently, where they were able to stretch out his contorted limbs. To seek the right documentation for the program, Nadia took Pasha to some doctors in the city, an hour and a half drive from Shishkino. In a hospital with no elevators, she hauled him up three flights of stairs. One doctor actually asked her why she cares for such a nobody as this.

Yet for Nadia, there is a simple answer. She is doing what God has called her to do and sees this as no great selfless act.

> Religion that God our Father accepts as pure and faultless is this: to look after orphans and widows in their distress.
>
> JAMES 1:27

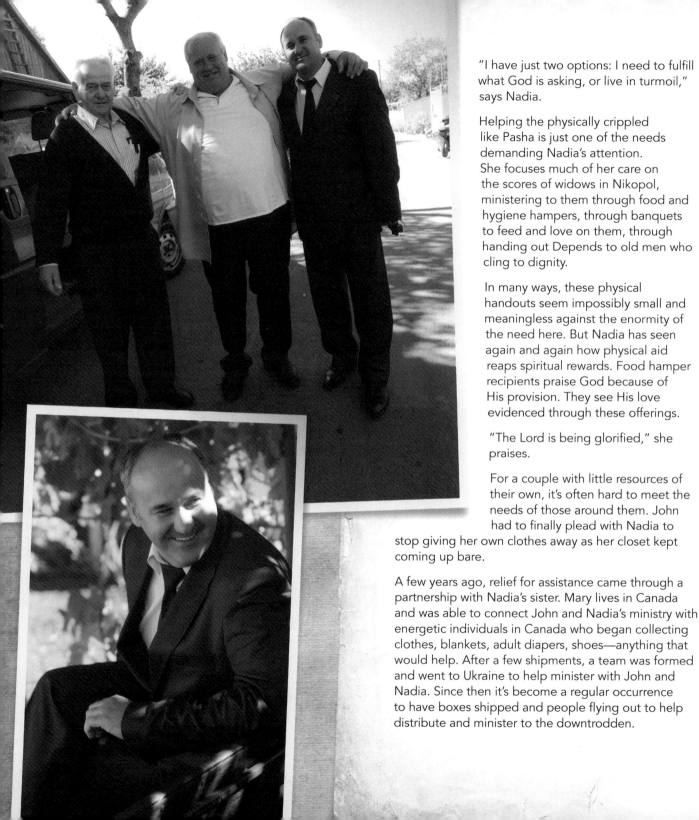

"I have just two options: I need to fulfill what God is asking, or live in turmoil," says Nadia.

Helping the physically crippled like Pasha is just one of the needs demanding Nadia's attention. She focuses much of her care on the scores of widows in Nikopol, ministering to them through food and hygiene hampers, through banquets to feed and love on them, through handing out Depends to old men who cling to dignity.

In many ways, these physical handouts seem impossibly small and meaningless against the enormity of the need here. But Nadia has seen again and again how physical aid reaps spiritual rewards. Food hamper recipients praise God because of His provision. They see His love evidenced through these offerings.

"The Lord is being glorified," she praises.

For a couple with little resources of their own, it's often hard to meet the needs of those around them. John had to finally plead with Nadia to stop giving her own clothes away as her closet kept coming up bare.

A few years ago, relief for assistance came through a partnership with Nadia's sister. Mary lives in Canada and was able to connect John and Nadia's ministry with energetic individuals in Canada who began collecting clothes, blankets, adult diapers, shoes—anything that would help. After a few shipments, a team was formed and went to Ukraine to help minister with John and Nadia. Since then it's become a regular occurrence to have boxes shipped and people flying out to help distribute and minister to the downtrodden.

"It is so important that teams are coming here," says John. "The more you devote yourself to the service of God, the more you see the needs."

John is better known as Pastor John. He is head of the Nikopol Baptist Church in Nikopol, and oversees approximately 30 church plants and Bible studies in communities surrounding the Nikopol District. John is focused on the state of people's relationship with the Lord. He is unconditionally selfless in his actions, his motives, his time.

He takes the Lord's Supper to those unable to come to the Lord's House. He hears of villages where no one is pastoring, where no Christians are working or where no support is coming. He seeks out the Christians there and supports as best he can, in places like Chkalovo. Money is tight in this town and when city workers are done at the factory, they head home to do hours of farm labour to keep the home-front running. People who live in Chkalovo face a hard life. And the church that John got started here is really helping the down-and-out in this community.

Luba lives in Chkalovo. Her husband suffers from a common affliction in this land—he's a terrible alcoholic. Adding to the tragedy, Luba's son left for the army and came back with mental problems.

"I was going crazy because of this; I can't express what a suffering it was," Luba shares.

Then a new neighbour moved in, a Christian woman. Together they went to Nikopol to go to church, and Luba's life was changed.

"The Holy Spirit touched me that day," she declares.

Luba knew she was missing something in her life and kept coming back to the church. After a month, she was ready and asked for repentance.

John's church and a short-term missions team renovated an old house in Chkalovo into a house church. Luba no longer has to try to find a ride or take the lengthy bus trip into Nikopol to attend church.

She's part of a Christian community in her own town, and here she finds support and encouragement to face the life set out before her.

John and Nadia are also connected to an orphanage in the town of Priazovskoje, about four hours away from Nikopol. With the help of Canadian teams, they are able to give food and clothing donations to the orphanage and funding for projects such as new windows, a new roof for the aging building, a workshop for boys and a sewing room for girls to learn life skills. And each time a team comes to Ukraine to work with John and Nadia's ministry, they take a trip to the orphanage to bless the children and encourage the Christians running the home.

Home visits, orphan care, widow ministry, spiritual guidance and physical aid are all part of John and Nadia's ministry. But to to look at what they are doing seems contradictory to who they are as individuals. For while they pour their hearts and souls into the people of Ukraine, they keep pointing the glory back to God.

"Our main goal is to share the Gospel with people, to tell people they can have eternal life with God," John says. For John and Nadia, there really is only one option in this life: to live for the glory of God.

Nadia works to clean up a men's rehab centre that's overseen by John.

A day at the clinic

It's hot and sunny on the day of the free medical clinic—typical Kenyan weather. Piled inside two vans are a doctor and pharmacist from Hillside Community Church in Coquitlam, B.C. and several others from the team to lend a hand. We pick up a small crew of nurses from the hospital in Siaya to do HIV testing. There is also a lab technician, a Hungry For Life leader, a photographer and a journalist.

We are quite the spectacle.

It's 10 a.m.

The day's plan: provide free medical care to as many Kenyans as possible out of a few bins of supplies in a basic two-room brick building.

We pull up to find dozens of people already waiting in clusters under the shade of a few trees.

There is much to do before the clinic opens. There's organizing of official medical cards and line-ups and translators. The doctor and pharmacist need to set up their temporary, primitive work stations in a room too small for the number of people that have to fit in. While bins are sorted, crowds begin to surge towards the building as though just getting close will ensure their chance at being treated today.

It's 10:30 a.m.

The people wait. Women rock eerily quiet babies, a surprising silence given many are here because their babies are sick. Men stand stoically. Small children dash between them playing simple games.

It's 11 a.m.

While waiting to see the lone doctor, patients go to the HIV testing stations set up around the perimeter of the grassy field. It isn't mandatory but many opt to take the test given the severely high rate of HIV and AIDS in Africa. According to the World Health Organization, 1.9 million people aquired the HIV virus in 2010 alone. An estimated 1.2 million Africans died of HIV-related illness in 2010, comprising a whopping 69 per cent of the global total of 1.8 million deaths.

A nurse talks to Nicholas.

It's 11:30 a.m.

Nicholas is one of the first patients to be tested. He looks younger than his 78 years, though the white bristles on his face reflect his true age. Nicholas has come to the clinic because he feels pain in his shoulders and back, and says his eyes are "wearing out" on him.

This is his first time being tested for HIV. A counsellor talks him through the procedure, first explaining how someone can contract HIV and methods of prevention.

Counsellor Sarah Atieno says sometimes people are shocked when they get the news. Others appear resigned even before learning the results, knowing the odds are stacked against them.

Nicholas sits down at one of the four stations, is pricked, and waits the few minutes it takes to find out his results—negative. He doesn't look surprised at the good result.

With a tattered white felt hat capping his head, Nicholas now waits patiently to see the doctor.

It's 12:00 p.m.

Team members take short breaks to make a sandwich in the van. Meanwhile, the hordes outside are hungry, and we wish we had the faith to pray that our loaves of bread would multiply to feed everyone here.

We drift through the crowd, listening to stories of moms with severe headaches, children with abdominal pain. An old woman who feels sick "all over her body," and is tired of waiting her turn. We hear of chest pains and sore necks. Rose suffers from diarrhea with blood in it and has constant stomachaches. Charles, who walked for half an hour to get here, has a wound on his foot from eight months ago that still hasn't healed. It looks disgusting.

It's 1:30 p.m.

The line is moving too slowly and people are tired and hungry. The sun continues to beat its steady ascent across the sky. It's hot and there is little shade for relief. But still they wait. Nicholas stands in line clutching his mandatory medical record book. Waiting.

It's 2:30 p.m.

The crowds have definitely swelled. There won't be enough time to see any of the latecomers. School is out of session now; kids crowd around the foreigners, demanding attention with calls of "mzungus" (white people).

It's 2:32 p.m.

Nicholas is called into the coveted building; he's watched with quiet envy by the sea of faces still waiting in the blistering sun. Things move faster now. Nicholas is inside the building, but still not in the room with the doctor. Through a translator, he must first tell a volunteer what ails him. She writes down the information so the doctor can quickly assess Nicholas instead of taking valuable minutes to gather preliminary details.

It's 2:44 p.m.

Nicholas is finally ushered into the doctor's 'office', the second room in the two-room building, light streaming in through the barred windows. Nicholas sits down, placing his felt hat in his lap as Dr. Kevin looks at Nicholas' record. He asks Nicholas to lift his arm up.

Kevin smiles.

"That's pretty good," he tells the aged man as he lifts his arm above his head.

As he works, Dr. Kevin shares that many of today's patients have aches and pains that can be attributed to the hard life they live.

"These people in their 60's and beyond, their bodies are just worn out," he explains.

They carry water for miles, they sleep on the dirt floor, they face malaria and heavy physical work. Food that's good for healthy bones and bodies is not readily available or affordable. Cars are not common and men like Nicholas, at close to 80 years old, walk an hour just to reach a free clinic. And all that takes a toll on the body. Dr. Kevin speculates that this patient probably has degenerative arthritis in his neck which means when he carries heavy objects such as a water jug, a sharp pain travels down his body.

It's possible from his symptoms listed that Nicholas also suffers from diabetes, but Dr. Kevin doesn't have the right equipment to test for that. There's only so

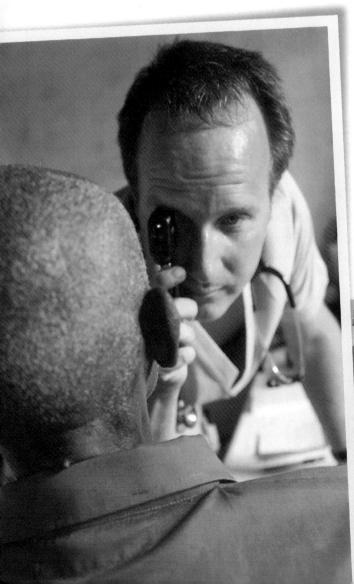

much you can bring in plastic totes packed in Canada without knowing what you'll face on clinic day.

Through the translator, Dr. Kevin murmurs to Nicholas that he will also check his eyes, reaching for a tool in a pile by his feet.

"I think your eyes are getting old," he tells Nicholas, adding there is no sign of cataracts.

Dr. Kevin prescribes a pain medication for his neck and shoulders.

"Thank you very much," Nicholas says in heavily-accented English as he gets up from the chair. The whole appointment lasts maybe five minutes.

It's 2:50 p.m.

Nicholas walks out of the building and through the teeming throngs waiting to see the doctor. Waiting for help. Waiting. He stands in the line for the pharmacist to fill his order through the barred windows of the building.

It's 3:05 p.m.

Nicholas gets his prescription filled: Acetaminophen, better known as Tylenol. Five hours of waiting. For Tylenol.

Was the wait worth it? Yes, Nicholas answers. He's in pain and is happy he has pills to take home, prescribed by a doctor and distributed for free.

"What has happened today is wonderful," Nicholas says. "I am grateful."

It's been a long day and Nicholas is ready to head back to his village.

It's 3:17 p.m.

He takes his bag of Tylenol, walks up the road a short distance, and heads onto an unmarked path to make his way home.

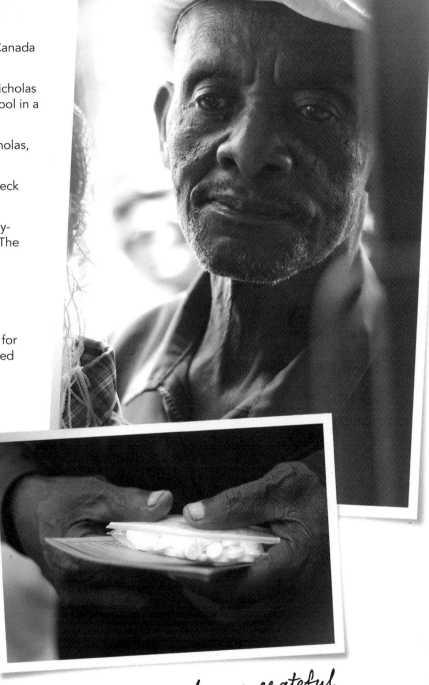

Nicholas leaves, grateful for the medicine.

Hillside Community Church, Coquitlam, B.C.

Now in their 5th year in Kenya, Hillside has finished their work in Boro and are now helping in the community of Seje.

Gene & Mai

The Couple

After 22 years of living in Waveland, Mississippi, Gene and Mai would still consider themselves newcomers. Waveland is one of those places where history takes precedence, where family ties connect you to the community. More than two decades here classifies Gene and Mai as settlers. It's nothing official, but perception is relevant.

They spent their married lives travelling the country for Mai's work as a consultant nurse. They lived in a few different places but when they found Waveland, a town of 9,000 located on the shores of the Gulf of Mexico, they knew this was a place they could call home.

They settled on a quiet suburban street in a trim yellow house. Hardwood floors feel cool against the muggy Mississippi air. Pale lemon curtains brush the kitchen window sill. In the living room, a shadow box holds Gene's WWII memorabilia from his time in the service.

Behind the house sits a matching yellow shed. Step inside and you're greeted by sunlight streaming through the single pane windows. Mai's beautiful paintings hang along the upper walls between animal heads collected over Gene's years of hunting. Vases filled with bristly paintbrushes rest on wooden benches and window ledges. Finished paintings and empty frames stack against the walls, jumbled together, spurts of colour bursting out from uncovered edges. Clearly, Mai's joy in life and her sense of exuberance transfers through her paintbrush onto canvas in this studio.

Mai was a city girl, raised in Memphis, Tennessee. Gene was a country boy. You look at this couple and imagine a fairytale beginning to their happy ending. You expect them to be high school sweethearts or young lovers who ventured out in a new life together. But Gene and Mai are human and they've both been thrown curveballs in this game of life. From separate marriages, Mai has three children and Gene has two.

When they met, Gene was living alone in a motel next to his restaurant. They met through a friend of a friend. Mai left a Gospel tract in his fridge and Gene read it late at night when all he was searching for was a glass of cold water, not salvation. He prayed if the Lord was really out there, if there was something to all of this, then he wanted to be a part of it. And Gene became a Christian that night.

Gene knows even before he was a Christian, God was watching out for him. He says he should've died "several times over" during the Second World War. He flew in the face of danger, working in the field with one of the highest death rates of any major branch in the war effort.

Gene and Mai have been happily married for almost 40 years now, and are as close now as they've ever been. Just sitting with this couple, you see the love and devotion they have for each other. On top of that, the love they have for Christ is obvious.

"The Lord Jesus Christ is responsible for taking care of our every need," Gene says. And that foundation has kept the Sanders secure even in rough waters.

The Storm

The 1969 hurricane was the reference point around here, with record level high waters marking the danger zone. Nothing before or after Hurricane Camille had ever hit those marks, so when the Sanders bought their home out of the flood zone in 1987, it was a safe bet they would stay high and dry during hurricane season.

In fact, when the warnings of a hurricane started coming in August 2005, some of their neighbours merely shrugged their shoulders. After all, Camille didn't come close, no way this one would either.

At the time, Mai was in the hospital waiting for a gall bladder operation. It was postponed and they left town. They always leave when a hurricane warning

Gene and Mai
in the backyard.

comes, with just a few clothes and a bathroom bag. In the slim chance the warning would actually turn into a real storm, they always packed their important papers and family pictures too.

The hurricane warning was nothing new. What was new was that no one was crying wolf this time. This time, it was Hurricane Katrina that hit. And she hit with a fury, attacking all who lay in her path. Katrina made Camille look like a puddle. Waveland was dubbed 'ground zero' and the destruction was shocking.

Gene came back after a week to a town absolutely destroyed.

"It was a total war zone," he recalls. The previous high water point was completely submerged, as were homes more than 20 kilometres inland.

The Sander's house was hit. Rain, wind, mud, water. It pummelled their house until there was not much left but a shell. The water came in and receded on the same day, leaving a thick cover of sludge. Mould quickly followed. The Sanders had 52 trees on their property; every single one of them is gone now, either ripped out during the hurricane or pulled down after because of their precarious positioning. He describes the devastation like "a tsunami." There wasn't a leaf left on a tree anywhere in sight.

Gene couldn't believe the destruction.

"You couldn't get in the house; everything was upside down," Gene recalls. "Half the ceiling had come down."

The Aftermath

It took thousands of volunteers to help clean up the mess. Relief camps sprung up overnight, with scores of volunteer teams coming to rebuild and repair.

The spirit in Waveland was one of help and care, Gene recalls. You couldn't buy anything, there were so many groups handing out food and clothing.

"They just kept coming. And the volunteers, they would do anything that needed to be done."

Mai stayed in Memphis for four months while Gene worked on salvaging their home. While the Sanders didn't have flood insurance, they were able to get some grants from the government to help cover repairs. Volunteer groups such as Camp Katrina assisted with everything from building floors to painting to cleaning.

Without the volunteers, Gene says it would have been nearly impossible to rebuild their home. It took a year, but the Sanders were finally able to move back in 2006.

But that's not the end of the story for the Sanders.

When they moved to Waveland, Gene and Mai were unable to find a church that felt like home. For awhile they did the one-hour drive to New Orleans for church, or sometimes would watch services on TV. When the hurricane hit, one volunteer group in particular helped Gene and Mai out. Camp Katrina volunteers stayed so long, they turned the camp into a permanent fixture in Waveland. They called it the Christian Life Center and began holding regular church services.

The Christian Life Center reaches out to the community through various ministries. Approximately 50 weeks of every year there is some form of a short-term missions team working through the center, helping to rebuild. The church hosts weekly coffee nights, providing a safe place to ask questions and build community. They run a thrift store, selling clothes and household items to people who cannot even afford to shop at low-cost department stores. And they have reached out to families like the Sanders, giving them a place to worship, to fellowship and—finally—to belong.

"It was an answer to prayer for us," says Mai. "We never would've met these people [if the hurricane hadn't happened]."

This couple's positive attitude simply cannot be dampened. It's a good thing too; their upbeat outlook has pulled them through experiences that are worse than hurricanes.

The Faith

Six years Mai ago had open heart surgery. She ended up having kidney failure and went into a coma. When she came out of the coma, she found her legs no longer working. Miraculously, her kidneys took over again. And Gene was able to teach her how to walk. Mai is now as mobile as anyone.

"That's God," she states. "I am truly in the hands of God."

And it turns out, Gene is now battling cancer. He doesn't cry about it. He simply asks for prayer.

Through everything, Gene and Mai have kept their positive attitude intact. They look realistically at the things that have happened in their life together—hurricanes, sickness and hardship—with the same God-focused eyes that examine their blessings—recovery, strength, and salvation.

And they're so thankful for what they've faced because it has helped them to become who they are today.

"We are blessed and tested and tried," says Gene. "It has to come for growth to happen."

A short-term missions team prays with Gene and Mai.

We took bags of bread to a poor house while in Mirebelais, Haiti with the team from Southside Church in Chilliwack.

As the men, women and children ate, I got to share my testimony. Out of all our travels, this is still one of my most powerful memories. It was humbling to meet some of the poorest of the poor; I pray we brought hope to them that day.

Christ & communism

It's a village you've definitely never heard of, near a city most of us will never go to, in a country that few travel to. But in the village of Vyschetarasivka, Ukraine, there is a story of a world transformed.

Brothers Michail and Vasiliy grew up in this small village about two hours outside Nikopol. Large smokestacks tower in the distant landscape, their emissions spreading a fine haze of pollution over the village.

For 70 years, residents here were told that communism was the answer and that God did not exist.

But God reaches out in even the darkest of places, and Michail became the very first Christian in his village of 3,700 more than 10 years ago. He prayed for his family; soon after, his brother Vasiliy became a Christian too. Together they planted a church and began the mission of reaching out to a truly lost people.

There are many challenges here. Some still believe God does not exist. Others follow the majority religion of the Ukraine, a religion of rules and regulations, not relationship. The brothers find it hard to witness: their neighbours—the people they grew up with—view Christianity as a cult. People here live day-to-day, focusing less on the state of their soul and more on their physical success. But the brothers persevere and believe that, through God, all things are possible.

We had the chance to visit Vyschetarasivka with a short-term missions team from Canada. While there, the team was able to bless the people with food and hygiene hampers. It's not much, but for the people here, the basic supplies can literally be a life-saver. Oksana was one of those who came for the hamper, and she was very grateful for the kindness of strangers. She walked for miles to come. She doesn't go to Michail and Vasiliy's church nor is she a Christian. We ask if she wants prayer.

"Pray that I have a good life," she requests.

Oksana tells us she feels all alone in this world. Her relatives are not on "good terms" with each other and her three-year-old son's father left her after seven months. She smiles at us, revealing her crooked teeth. Then she bends down and hugs her son and takes him to play with the new toys he was given.

Michail and Vasiliy know it is in these types of gestures that their community will be reached. To show kindness to women like Oksana caught in a world of hurt shows God's love more than all the sermons in the world. They persevere, praying that women like Oksana will return to the church's doorstep next Sunday even though this time there will be no food to hand out.

For Vasiliy and Michail, their biggest prayers were answered when both their wives became believers and now their children have followed the same path.

"I have nothing to dream for anymore," Vasiliy says with contentment.

Ten years after the church was planted, there are now nine adult members and a few more that attend on a regular basis. It's a tiny church, fitting a maximum of 20 inside its white, plastered walls. Yes, it's small. But the Christians in Vyschetarasivka are filled with the joy of the Lord as they happily worship together with fellow Christians from across the world.

Oksana and her cute kid.

Cowboy Pastor

It's hard to find someone worth following. There's a lack of substance in the men and women we place above us. Celebrities, rulers, local politicians—most lack the ability to gain trust.

Yet there are leaders worth following, if you look in the right place. Look, for example, in Mexico and to Pastor Tomas. He is a man of strength, a man of vision, and a man of action. He has a strong passion for the unreached and hard-to-access indigenous people of Mexico, the Tarahumara Indians.

The Tarahumara live hidden from the world's eyes in craggy rock enclaves in the depths of the Copper Canyon. When the Spanish conquistadors attacked and tried to turn the indigenous population into slaves, the Tarahumara fled to the canyon to escape persecution. They have lived there ever since, afraid of the outside world and slowly starving to death.

Pastor Tomas lives in the same country as the Tarahumara, but in a totally different world. He is the head pastor of a large Alliance church in Juarez, Mexico, and has established a growing ministry in the troubled border city.

One day he was watching TV and saw a story about an entire civilization of people dying of starvation.

"I felt a huge need in front of me when I found out they were becoming extinct," says Pastor Tomas. "I decided to make a trip; I wanted to see it with my own eyes."

When he arrived at the first village, there was a funeral underway and he asked what had happened. They told him the man died of hunger.

"I felt a deep sadness, to know that someone can die just because he didn't have a little corn. That brought a huge burden to me. I remember I prayed to God that I could come at least once a month to bring food to these people. I think God took my word on that."

He figured out it would cost roughly $1,000 to make the trip into the canyon every month with food to distribute; his church in Juarez simply did not have that kind of money.

With no funding but a heart of anguish, Pastor Tomas humbled himself before the Lord with this burden. And somehow, the funding has come to conduct ongoing mission trips into the Copper Canyon. It has flourished into a full ministry, reaching out to communities further and further from civilization.

"I felt a deep sadness, to know that someone can die just because he didn't have a little corn."

Pastor Tomas and his team bring basic necessities such as food and clothing to the famished and freezing in Mexico. People come to receive and Pastor Tomas takes the opportunity to meet with them face to face. He speaks of the love of Christ and demonstrates it by providing for their physical needs. 'Pastor', as he is affectionately called, saves people from death by starvation and death without salvation.

"Our principal goal is that everybody know Jesus, the Saviour," he says with a quiet and heartfelt voice. His weathered face reveals the years of trekking through the elements to reach far-flung destinations, and his attire is simple and practical—a cowboy pastor in the heart of Mexico.

"I want to live; not to think of the cost, but to go to those places that have more needs," he shares. "This doesn't come automatically. You have to walk, to stumble, to feel you're sometimes not able to go on and then you can see God there…If I didn't see God walking in front of me, I wouldn't go."

Pastor Tomas is a man worth following, because he follows in God's footsteps.

Testimony at gunpoint

One day Pastor Tomas was travelling on his own through the Copper Canyon. He was forced to stop in a village he had never been to because the snow was so high he couldn't travel anymore.

While he was staying there, Pastor Tomas began sharing his faith with the residents. It turns out, the town was run by a drug lord and most people in the community worked for him. But when people began hearing about Christ, they wanted to give up their lives in the drug industry.

"The mayor of the little town accepted Jesus, and every day I started seeing people come to Christ. It was wonderful to see."

One evening a man asked Pastor Tomas to come outside the village with him. He thought the man wanted prayer or to talk about Christ away from other people, so Pastor Tomas complied.

But when they got out of town, the drug lord and a circle of armed men were waiting to greet him. They told Pastor Tomas he was hurting their business in town and they were going to kill him.

Pastor Tomas asked the men that, if they were going to kill him anyway, to give him five minutes to speak. After five minutes of sharing, the men were in tears. Convicted, they asked Pastor Tomas to pray with them and told him he could leave town and just keep doing what he was doing.

"I'm sure God did something in their hearts that day," Pastor Tomas says. "What really touched my life was to see how God worked in their lives."

Don

Don is a hardworking, salt-of-the-earth type of guy. He's worked all his life and, at 65, he's still a working man. He never saw himself going on a missions trip but a woman from his church knew his skills and his heart, and told him to go to Mexico.

Don lives and works on the water's edge, in a beautifully messy stretch of land found on Kitmat's fjord shores. The landscape is more scrapyard than ocean front, dark shades of metal and wood jumbled together under salty skies.

Don is a tinkerer and tradesman, and was building a tugboat from scratch when we met with him.

He went to Mexico with his church, Mountainview Alliance. And what he found there took him by surprise. Don had always figured people could pull themselves up by their own bootstraps and better their lives. Now he was seeing kids that had no schooling, no job opportunities and no food and hearing stories of many in this tiny village dying of starvation. And it broke him up.

Don got to be a part of something larger than his own life during that trip to Mexico. It opened up his world, giving him perspective on the hurt and the struggle facing the poor in Mexico's Copper Canyon.

Don comes from a small church in a small town out of the way of anywhere. But through their connection to Mexico, Don is part of something that is changing lives.

"Every Christian should forget his age and just go where the Lord sends him," Don urges.

Elisabeth

Elisabeth's passion for prayer mobilized an entire church to cover its short-term missions team in prayer. When her church in the small town of Kitimat, B.C. began sending teams to Mexico, Elisabeth organized a prayer list. Church members got behind the idea and readily signed up under Elisabeth's watchful gaze. Even a six-year-old girl asked if she could be part of the prayer team.

"I was so excited to see the Lord is calling her to prayer," Elisabeth comments.

The first trip's success fueled the desire in the church to build a strong relationship with the partner in Mexico. Now, Elisabeth finds many prayer warriors, especially those who have gone to Mexico and seen the good work happening under their project partner Pastor Tomas.

But Elisabeth is also thankful to see that prayer volunteers include people who have not gone to Mexico, yet are standing behind the church's call to missions. By facilitating prayer teams, Elisabeth has helped foster a missional heart in Mountainview Alliance Church.

"I really felt like I was supposed to," Elisabeth says. "The thing that I wanted was to allow the people in the church to be part of something where they could really pray specifically and see God answer…it was about causing people to trust God more, to believe that He answers prayer."

Kitimat's missions are covered in prayer.

Ruby

With no phone service available, we show up to Ruby and Enrique's home unannounced. Ruby's contagious smile reveals her joy at these unexpected visitors. We're here with Nancy, one of the Por Amor Foundation volunteers based in the city of Manta, Ecuador. Rapidly speaking in Spanish, Ruby says she dreamt someone from this family-based organization would come soon and she had been waiting in anticipation.

Ruby excitedly hugs Nancy again and again, a broken-toothed smile stretching across her gaunt face.

She finally settles down and we move inside her home to listen to Ruby's story.

Hers is a sad tale. As a child, Ruby was abandoned by her mother. Another woman took her in but her own children abused Ruby. She was raped by the guard at the elementary school she attended.

"My life was very sad until I met Enrique," she says. He and Ruby have been together more than a dozen years now and have two children, Enrique and Jennifer.

Ruby has coped daily with epilepsy, a disorder that controls her life. For several months, she was under the care of Catholic nuns at a hospital for the terminally ill. Enrique had to keep working and with no family living here, their two young children were left home alone. A social worker at the hospital heard about the dilemma and called her friend Pearl to see if there was anything they could do to help.

Nancy's daughter and son-in-law, Pearl and Allan Jackson, are the directors of the Por Amor Foundation. The Jacksons didn't know the family, but willingly opened their home to care for the children while Ruby was in the hospital.

"She wasn't ready to die, but she was very sick," Nancy explains as we sit at the rough wooden table. "We would go take the children on weekends to see their mother. This lasted for two or three months."

Finally Ruby was able to go home, and the Jacksons saw another way they could help this struggling family. Their ramshackle home was made of very thin slats of bamboo tied together; a tin sheet and ripped black tarp formed the roof. Por Amor was able to help Ruby and Enrique acquire land, where government-assisted housing projects are rising from the dusty ground. Their new brick and concrete home might be small by North American standards, but is a huge blessing to Enrique and Ruby. It's sturdy, it doesn't leak in the rain and there is a solid roof over their heads. Security is found in the metal bars covering the windows, and plastic sheeting acts as a privacy curtain.

"We're thankful to God for our home," Ruby declares.

And they're very thankful for the Jacksons and Por Amor.

"They're the only real family we have," Enrique reflects.

Pastor William

Pastor William is a hardworking, dedicated pastor in one of the poorest areas of Kenya. In a country of little, Pastor William has nothing.

His church meets outside, guarded from the beating Kenyan sun under the shade of a yellow oleander tree. They don't have a building. But they have a lot of heart and spirit. People in Segere are drawn into the love of Christ through the Holy Spirit at work in this tiny African enclave.

His vehicle is a rickety, rusty bicycle. When his bike is broken and there's no money to repair it, William walks to Segere to lead his flock. It takes two hours, one way. His wife and four children come with him, walking the dusty roads. On Sundays, the family doesn't eat because there's no time to return home between services and no one in the church can afford to feed them.

After becoming a pastor, William felt called to Segere as his mission field.

"I heard God's voice to start a church there," he explains.

He spent three months going from hut to hut, door to door, preaching God's Word and reaching out to the lost and lonely. Many have come to know Christ through William's preaching, including Lillian Awino.

He walks two hours
to get to church.

Lillian had heard the Gospel before but it never meant anything to her. When Pastor William came to her house and shared, she was ready and responded whole-heartedly.

"I'm a new creature. I was healed," she shares.

She's now part of a gardening program that is turning infertile soil into miracle patches of healthy-growing produce. Through a Canadian-funded program, local pastors have been trained in bio-intensive organic farming and have in turn trained people in their communities. Pastor William learned the techniques from his friend and mentor Pastor Michael, and is now in turn training four people in Segere.

It doesn't mean life is much easier for William with this new training. Right now his children are unable to go to school as he doesn't have enough money to pay the school fees. With no water source nearby, William and his children walk approximately two hours round trip to get water; they do that four times a day. His 11-year-old daughter Elizabeth shows us proudly how she carries the jugs: one on her head, the other on her hip.

It's frustrating when you start to look at monumental problems like hunger and starvation in Africa. In Kenya alone, more than 22 million people are facing conditions of extreme poverty. The number is staggering. But it will be family by family, hut by hut, that this number will drop. Pastor William, his trainee Lillian, and others in the small village of Segere are learning how to grow results-giving gardens. Each family taking part in this program now has enough to feed their own families and some even sell produce at the market, bringing in much-needed income. It might not help 22.8 million, but the training is having an impact on one pocket of Kenya and is taking that number down a notch, thanks to men like Pastor William.

Elizabeth gathers water while Steve helps his dad in the garden.

The Kumaris

In our 'believe-what-you-want society', it might be hard to imagine living in a country based solely on religious rule. But if you go to Sri Lanka, there's only one religion that really counts for anything. The numbers confirm it; of 21.3 million citizens, approximately 70 per cent are Buddhist.

There's a smattering of Muslims, Hindus and Christians. But none comes close to the amount of Buddhists. Like other highly religious countries, there's no separation of church and state here.

Sunil and Anusha Kumari, Buddhists living in the heart of Sri Lanka, never really questioned their religion. When you live in a country where seven out of every 10 people follow the same beliefs, it's just part of life.

But if they had to pick who is on their side during hard times, Sunil and Anusha would not choose the Buddhists. Nor would they choose the Hindus or the Muslims.

They would choose the Christians.

The Kumaris had been married for almost 20 years. Their house, which they shared with their two sons, was in desperate need of renovations. However, they had no money for repairs and the bank wouldn't give them a loan. They went several times to the Buddhist temple for help but were never offered assistance.

"We didn't have a proper room to live in," Anusha shares. "There were branches that were supporting the roof…There were no windows, no doors. We kept animals out by covering the door frame and window frame with plastic."

A Christian pastor, Ranjan Fernando, was in the Kumari's village a few years ago running a mobile medical clinic when he first heard about the Kumari's plight.

"I felt very sorry for them," Ranjan recalls. "They couldn't even offer water to me when I came to visit."

Ranjan found Sunil and Anusha assistance through a non-profit housing group. After the renovations, the Kumaris now have a brand new roof, new walls, doors, an additional room, a kitchen, a well and even a bathroom.

"It was like a dream to us. It was a miracle," says Sunil.

They used to walk a two-hour round trip to gather water for drinking and household use. Now they can go outside and pull up buckets of fresh water from their well.

"We are grateful," says Sunil. "Life is a little better now."

Sunil and Anusha find it hard to articulate why Ranjan and his Christian organization helped them.

"Why are Christians so different?" Sunil questions. As if trying to answer his own query, he concludes, "There is something…"

Now the Kumaris get frustrated when they see the Buddhist monks living within the temple walls, well-fed and provided for by the working poor who reside in the surrounding communities.

"We must go to the temple and we must give," explains Sunil. "But the Christians would come to us. They come and see us and want to know about us. That is new to us."

They have seen the difference between Buddhists and Christians. And while they haven't changed their religion—yet—it's obvious something is going on in their hearts to make them reconsider the dominant religion in Sri Lanka.

"Buddhism is a beautiful story," says Sunil. But, he adds, "it is not much more than that."

"The Christians are concerned about the poor. It's a new experience. We see [Christianity] not only by talking mouths, but by example. By action."

"The Christians are
concerned about the poor.
It's a new experience."

Yoni

Trained as a nurse, Yoni first came on board at ATEK to help with health campaigns. She travelled into the Cusco region countryside to teach people about parasites. One thing led to another, and Yoni ended up coming on staff at ATEK full-time.

ATEK is an interdenominational Christian organization working to strengthen the Cusco-Quechua people living in the region surrounding Cusco, Peru. Through literacy programs people are learning to read the Bible in their own language. Through marriage seminars couples are learning how to treat each other better. Through discipleship training pastors are learning how to lead their communities. Through audio-visual programs people are hearing the Gospel in their own Quechua language.

Yoni is now in charge of training Sunday School teachers in the villages. In Quechua communities there's a belief that children aren't important, that they don't belong in church. In the workshops, Yoni shows adults through the Bible that kids are important and they are an integral part of any church body.

Since starting the Sunday School training, Yoni has seen an impact where it matters: the kids. Early on, the children wouldn't talk to her as they were scared of outsiders. Now, Yoni says, the kids are full of confidence.

"They receive me with a smile and a hug."

She's seen many children come to Christ, and many adults gaining confidence as they learn how to lead Sunday School. While she spends her days ministering to the Quechua people, she never considered herself a missionary.

"I always thought missionaries had to leave their country and go somewhere else," she comments.

But Yoni, who is also Quechua, is clearly ministering and working to bring salvation to this largely unreached people. At only 24 years old, Yoni has found God's calling on her life here at ATEK. However, that doesn't mean life is easy for Yoni; working at ATEK has its challenges.

She travels long distances, often in overcrowded trucks or by motorcycle along "roads"—dirt tracks cut from the steep mountainsides, sheer cliffs on one side and a rising, unprotected mountain on the other. She makes little money, is out of Cusco for days at a time and faces many obstacles in the Sunday School training program. But for Yoni, the rewards are worth the suffering.

"It's like the Bible says, if you draw near to Him and make yourself available to what He would have you do, He will show you great things," Yoni says. "And He will do great things through you."

Yoni surrounded by the kids in Huanca Huanca.

New arrivals

The police station in Mukono, Uganda, is no place for children. It is a rusted metal shack, hot and dusty, and barely has room for the handful of people crammed in here trying to figure out the future of two small babies.

Yet here they sit, one in the arms of a despondent woman sitting quietly in a splintered wooden chair. The other rests in the arms of a policewoman while she fills out the necessary paperwork.

This is the beginning of a new life for these children, as their care is transferred from their aunt and uncle into the loving arms of Noah's Ark Children's Home, run by Piet and Pita Butendijk.

It often happens this way, says Pita. They get a call from the police station asking if they have room for another child. There's no government social welfare system and no other orphanages in the area. So when a young child is abandoned in Mukono, the police turn to Noah's Ark. They have yet to turn away a child.

"There's always room in the inn," Pita tells us.

Noah's Ark is a home for the children others have discarded. A place where the unwanted are wanted, where the unloved are loved again. In the middle of a desperate country sits a home filled with hope as children are given a second chance at life. Here, they are cared for, shown love, provided an education and given the opportunity to grow up stronger than their own parents were, whatever the circumstances they come from.

These twin brothers were born to a 19-year-old woman. But she got sick and died. The father is nowhere to be found, a common occurrence in Uganda. The police tell us they search for fathers of abandoned children, but Pita is doubtful anything will come of it.

"I'm waiting for many fathers," she says skeptically.

The boys' aunt and uncle took in the babies. But with six children of their own, their finances are already stretched. Their uncle has no interest in keeping them and told his wife they had to go.

Time is spent discussing the care the babies have received. Have they been immunized? What kind of milk were they

Noah's Ark is a home for the children others have discarded.

fed? Is the proper paperwork for them filled out?

Finally, the moment arrives. The babies have been transferred officially to Noah's Ark. Pita carefully picks them up and walks from the dark interior to the bright Ugandan sun outside. We get in the truck to leave, Pita carrying the precious cargo in her arms.

The aunt, who has shown no emotion and barely said a word the whole time we're inside, stands at the entrance. She watches the truck back out of the station and into the road. And as we pull away, I can see her wiping hot tears from her dusty face. The last evidence of her sister, the final gift of life she brought, is now entrusted to total strangers.

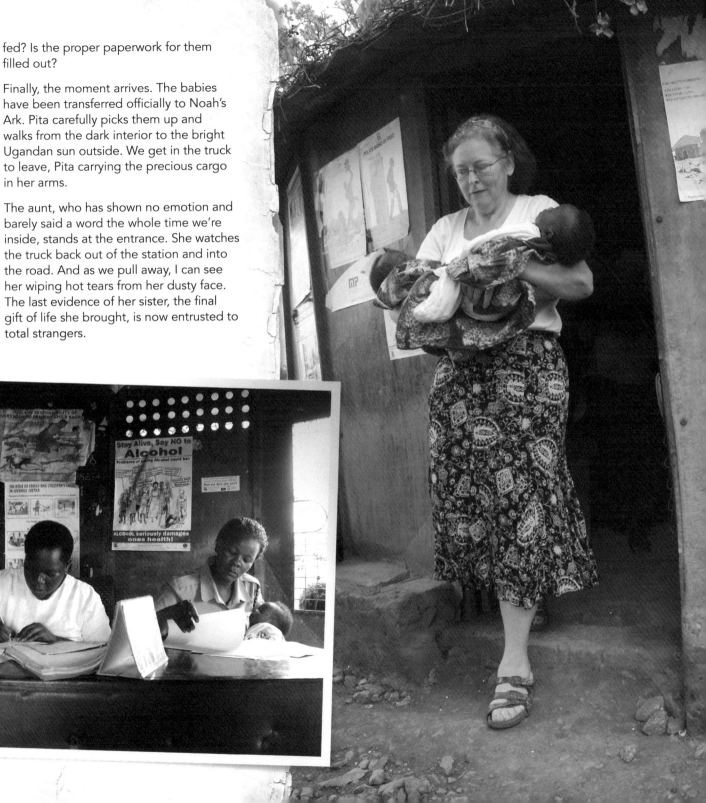

But the boys will be well cared for here. They will grow up at Noah's Ark having never known another life. By Sunday, they've been oohed and awed over by dozens of children, they've been fed and clothed and bathed, and appear well on their way to settling into their new home. And they are given names.

At Sunday's service, the children are embraced into this large and loving family with a dedication in prayer. Welcome home, Zeke and Theodore, you will be loved here.

The twins getting some much needed love in their new home.

Frances

Frances could stay home, enjoying her prairie view while reading a good book and keeping company with her 20-pound orange cat, Toby. Pictures of her late husband, four children and nine grandchildren show a life fully lived.

Certainly no one at Springbank Community Church expected her to sign up for a short-term missions trip. After all, teams face long hours, uncomfortable situations, hot temperatures, unfamiliar surroundings and, quite often, hard labour when they go the the mission field.

But God gave Frances a passion and purpose since the passing of her husband. She knows his death has allowed her to be fully available,"with a capital A," she exclaims. So Frances went on her church's first missions trip to Noah's Ark Children's Home in Uganda.

It was a memorable experience to say the least. She recalls the sad stories of how children end up at the orphanage, like a baby found wrapped in a plastic bag, his umbilical cord still attached. Or the girl who was raped and bore a child when she was still a child herself.

But she also remembers the way the children are now, living under the umbrella of care the orphanage provides. They play happily, running and laughing like children should. They eat healthy meals. They are cared for and loved. And they sing praises to Jesus.

"They have been through such terrible experiences, and still they sing about God," she says. "Every child there is a miracle."

And for this grandmother, the joy in serving on a missions trip was found in the hugs, the cuddles, the wiping of noses and tears, and sharing of laughter and play with the many abandoned kids who now have a permanent, safe and loving home.

The partnership with Noah's Ark has been a good fit for Springbank Community Church, located in a small affluent community just outside Calgary, Alberta. While money is easily raised in this church, having people give of their time by actually going to Africa has been a faith-building exercise for many. Frances is now one of the many passionate advocates for short-term missions.

"I would like to see a lot more people go and experience it, to see another way of life," she concludes.

Certainly no one expected her to sign up for a short-term missions trip.

Edward

Edward Fyodorov was a loathsome, dangerous, drug-addicted criminal. At least that's how he describes himself.

But there were other words to describe him too. Lost. Hopeless. Stuck in a life of addiction. For more than 20 years, living in a small Ukrainian town, Edward was a drug user. Trapped in a life that robbed him of everything close to him. Friends died, his family disowned him. He even lost his wife who died of a drug overdose.

Edward says he was the worst of sinners, like Paul writes in 1 Timothy 1:15b: "Christ Jesus came into the world to save sinners—of whom I am the worst."

"People sealed me as the person without hope," Edward utters, looking at me with kind brown eyes. "Everybody who would look at me would say I am a dead person."

His tale begins in much the same way as others who become lost. Edward started using drugs when he was 15 years old. At first it was just something "interesting" to try. And then he couldn't live without it.

On top of his drug use, he also became an unfaithful husband, constantly cheating on his wife. Edward continued to abuse his body, holding fast to the grand delusion of the addicted: to continue, even when all signs point to a destructive end.

Because of his lust for drugs, Edward was often in trouble with the law. And one day it all came crashing down on him. Edward got into a very serious fight with a policeman and a lawsuit was started against him.

With the court date looming, Edward got drunk and ended up in another fight. He was on the losing end; he wound up in the hospital for more than a month of recovery.

But the direction of his life changed when an old friend of Edward's happened on him in the hospital. He had come to see another person staying in the same room. When Alexi walked in, he immediately recognized Edward. Alexi's wife and Edward had known each other since they were children. Both she and Alexi had been drug addicts, and she'd landed in prison a few times. But ten years before Edward ended up in the hospital, Alexi was in the same place on his deathbed with tuberculosis of the bones. A local church prayed over him; he was healed and gave his life to Christ.

> Edward was a loathsome, dangerous, drug-addicted criminal. At least that's how he describes himself.

Here is a trustworthy saying that deserves full acceptance: Christ Jesus came into the world to save sinners—of whom I am the worst.

1 TIMOTHY 1:15

Edward hard at work at the men's rehab centre.

Edward with Pastor Nikoli and some of the men going through rehab.

After his conversion, Alexi really seemed to be a different guy. He was happier, and whenever they ran into each other, Alexi would invite Edward over to his house to share how God changed his life. But Edward always replied that he was fine the way he was. Now here he was in the hospital, a sobering consequence of the life he was still living while Alexi had turned his around. Yet Alexi did not condemn him.

"He didn't say a word of rebuke to me."

Alexi volunteered to bring food and clothing to Edward, and told him that whether he wanted it or not, Alexi's church was going to pray for him.

"And I'm telling you," Edward retells Alexi's words: "You're going to be a great preacher, you're going to have a changed life some day."

Edward didn't believe him. He was sure it was too late to turn his life around. But after Alexi left, Edward starting thinking about his life.

"I realized I didn't have happiness, I didn't have joy. Alexi was always energetic, always happy. And I didn't have that."

Alexi had left a New Testament with Edward and he began to read it. Meanwhile, the lawsuit case was on hold while Edward was in the hospital. The judge came to see him there to make sure his injuries were not a lie. She told Edward he couldn't continue life like this, that he had to change. Two different people coming to Edward with care and concern struck a chord and got Edward thinking. At his court hearing, Edward told the judge he knew he needed to change, and that after reading the Bible he realized he needed to repent. He said he planned to start going to church.

Because of the crime, Edward expected to be "severely" punished with the minimal sentence being five years in prison. But, Edward says, "God was merciful and I didn't end up in prison at all."

Edward had grown up only 15 metres from a church, but descriptively says he had to go through Mongolia to get there.

"I came to the church then and they accepted me," he says. "They knew me since I was a child, and they had been praying for me."

Edward repented and six months later was baptized. Three years later, we meet him working at a Christian-based rehabilitation centre. The home is for men recovering from drug addiction. It was started by a man named Pastor Nikoli (who has since passed away).

"The main idea is to give them hope. In this world, everybody has rejected them," Edward shares. "But they need to understand that their happiness is not dependent upon the surrounding circumstances, but on their inner parts."

He loves working with the men. With his experiences, Edward is able to help in ways others simply couldn't.

"God gave this grace to me, and now I'm alive by His grace. So I just want to share. And you know? I can give them something," he says proudly.

The rehab centre Edward works at was in such rough shape, Christians in Canada have raised money to build a new home for 16 recovering addicts. The grand opening was expected to take place in the summer of 2012.

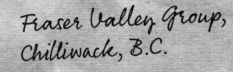

Fraser Valley Group,
Chilliwack, B.C.

This team traveled
to Nikopol, Ukraine
to feed, clothe and
minister to widows
and orphans. They
also renovated
a church.

Sterling

Sterling is dressed smart in a dark blue suit, a crisp white shirt and a conservative tie. His black face glistens in the afternoon sun, his ivory smile crinkling well-worn paths from the edge of his eyes to his temples.

Sterling is a Haitian working to help end poverty in Haiti. This might seem an impossible task; 80 per cent of the population lives below the poverty line with 54 per cent living in abject poverty. But Sterling looks beyond to the possibility that, with God involved, all things are possible.

He's committed to an organization based in Grand Goâve, Haiti, that works to train Haitians with practical skills, enabling them to succeed in a country with more than 80 per cent unemployment. For Sterling, being the administrator of the Haiti ARISE school is more than just a job. It's a way to help Haitians get out of the depths of despair many in this country face. Sterling is in charge of helping young men and women to be raised up in faith and in education. Students are learning valuable job skills in areas as diverse as mechanics, woodworking and pastoral training.

He can identify with those under his care. After all, Sterling was born and raised in Grand Goâve, and he loves this community with a deep passion. He was not a Christian when Haiti ARISE was established less than 10 years ago, but was drawn in by a free music class offered at the compound. While there, he was told about Jesus Christ and knew that was what he had been searching for. Sterling became a Christian, and was so impacted by the experience, he went on to take administrative classes so he could come back as a trained professional to work at Haiti ARISE.

Haiti ARISE Director Marc Honorat says it's a real blessing to have a local filling this role instead of short-term missionaries who come and go. Sterling is here to stay. For the first year Sterling worked, there was not even enough funding to be able to pay him. But his dedication was not to the paycheque, it was to the organization. He sometimes works so many hours he has to be reminded to go home and sleep.

Something as simple as free music lessons led Sterling to become a Christian, turning the commonplace into the extraordinary. And now he sees that same power at work in the students of his school. In a country full of indifference, Sterling stands out as a dedicated Christian committing to repairing his country, one trained student at a time.

Sterling is a Haitian working to help end poverty in Haiti.

Sydnee has travelled to Haiti many times for short-term missions trips through her church, Southside, in Chilliwack, B.C. But each time, she learns something new and knows that God has called her once again to serve the Haitian people.

"I loved getting out in the community. It was amazing to go hear people's life stories and get the chance to just talk to and pray with them."

Sydnee has learned a lot about her own faith, and knows she needs to give everything to God.

—Sydnee, Southside Church, Chilliwack, B.C.

From nobody to somebody

Uganda is overrun with orphans. AIDS has taken a devastating toll on parents, leaving children to fend for themselves. Sexually abused women leave unwanted babies in garbage cans and fields. Teenage pregnancies, poverty and a lack of support systems result in thousands of orphans.

Everyone knows change needs to happen, but how? Where do you begin in a country of more than 2.2 million orphans?

For the community of Mukono, Uganda, change is happening one life at a time. One orphan off the street, one child in school, one job for a father. There are many individual stories. But added together, they form a picture of a community transformed—one life at a time.

The driving force behind this change is Noah's Ark Children's Home. This organization is bringing hope to a destitute region of Uganda.

Piet and Pita Butendijk are the visionaries behind Noah's Ark. They saw the scores of orphans and knew they had to do something. Noah's Ark began in 2001 with a rental house and a few abandoned children. They quickly outgrew that space and in 2006 moved to their current location—a sprawling compound with room for expansion surrounding the spacious main house. Beginning here with 55 children, that number doubled within three years. And there always seems to be another child in need.

For 130 orphans, Noah's Ark has become a safe refuge. A home. If you were to watch most of these kids running, playing, laughing and crying, you might suspect they're just like any other kids. In some ways they are. But start reading through their profiles and you get a whole different picture.

Their stories are heartbreaking.

The children all have traumatic pasts, including abandonment, loss of both parents, cruel treatment, mental and physical abuse, even rape.

Piet and Pita saw scores of orphans and knew they had to do something.

A baby girl born in December 2005 was literally thrown away. Young children playing nearby found the tiny baby and brought her to the police station. Noah's Ark took in this unwanted child, who was so cold the thermometer did not even register a temperature. They named her Noelle.

Now, she is a bubbly three-year-old full of life and happiness. She is so cheerful, they have added to her original name. The girl who was thrown away is now known as Noelle Joy and she is flourishing in this environment of care and compassion. There are 129 more stories just like hers.

To see children who have gone through such trauma and at a glance seem just like any other child is proof of the love given here. Their motto, 'From Nobody to Somebody', fits well.

Still, it's not enough for Piet and Pita to put a roof over an orphan's head. Noah's Ark has also opened an elementary school on the grounds.

The New Horizons Nursery and Primary School is one of the most noticeable ways

↖ Noelle Joy.

Noah's Ark is transforming the community. After the school was built, classrooms were filled with students from the poorest families found in the surrounding villages. Of the 225 students, two-thirds come from outside the Noah's Ark gate every morning.

Young brothers Mugisha and Elvis had no chance of ever going to school. Books, uniforms and other school fees were too costly for a family living a life of subsistence. Their father died of AIDS two years ago, and now their mother Nanono has this sickness too.

"I didn't have any hope to take my children to school," she utters.

Nanono, who looks much older than her 23 years of age, has no job skills and no means of employment. The family's main food staple is cassava, a vegetable she grows in a small patch beside their mud hut home.

Mugisha, 11, and Elvis, 8, walk several hours each day for the privilege to attend school. There, they are fed a nutritious breakfast and lunch, their books are paid for and they're given a solid education.

Nanono knows going to school will help not only Mugisha and Elvis, but her three younger children as well. Education makes all the difference here. It means Mugisha and Elvis will have opportunities to learn a trade, to earn a living, to know their rights as Ugandans and to provide for their family.

"Whatever assistance they're getting will make a big difference for my children," Nanono asserts.

The level of education is low here in Mukono, with less than half of all eligible children enrolled in school. Through this project, Noah's Ark is helping a very vulnerable population. Most of the students coming to school from the community have lost at least one parent. Many live with elderly grandparents who can barely take care of themselves let alone a child.

"Such a person cannot raise money for school fees," Headmaster Sam Nsereko says. "With huge families some cannot even afford paraffin to light their house, or they cannot afford to buy a kilo of sugar."

As students graduate from lower grades, Noah's Ark has built classrooms to accomodate secondary students and vocational training in a post-secondary environment.

In some ways, the school is having an immediate impact in the community. Children are healthier, they're being fed and they're learning. But in many ways, the impact of this project won't be seen for many years— not until students start graduating with job skills and can contribute back to their own family's well-being.

Nanono knows that the education will benefit her whole family.

One of Noah's Ark's newest projects is perhaps seeing the most immediate and widespread impact. In September 2009, they opened a clinic on the Noah's Ark grounds. The clinic does everything from examinations and surgery to dental services and even village outreaches where they provide health education and services. They have an on-site lab service and pharmacy, and treat infants to adults. However, the primary focus of this clinic is to help pregnant women.

According to the United Nations, maternal health indicators for Uganda have remained generally poor for the last two decades. The UN estimates that for every 100,000 live births, there are 505 women who die. On top of that, the report cites that only 41 per cent of births overall in Uganda are attended by a

skilled professional. So if anything goes wrong, there's no one there to deal with complications.

The Noah's Ark team hopes if more women have proper care during pregnancy and labour, they will be more likely to not die during childbirth and leave another orphan on the streets.

Noah's Ark has built transitional homes for older children. Here, they learn how to live in a smaller family environment and receive more focused attention from house parents. There's the village outreach initiatives, where Noah's Ark kids connect with community grandparents, to learn about Ugandan culture. There's the students from the villages who learn about things like sanitation at school and bring those lessons home to their families, creating healthier family units. There's the parents who are learning for free after school how to read and write so they can turn around and help their own children. There's the more than 100 jobs that have been created with the building up of Noah's Ark Children's Home and New Horizons Primary School. But all these projects have one aim.

"Every project we do is geared towards closing the children's home," Piet says. All these projects focus on raising up educated, healthy and strong families who will raise their own children. One day, the Butendijks would love to close down the orphanage. They would love it if every mother who gave birth was able to keep her child. Their dream is a Uganda with stable families caring for their own children.

But until that happens, Noah's Ark will continue to provide for the orphans left in garbage cans and fields, abandoned by relatives or left alone by a dying mother. And they will continue expanding to be able to provide for their 130, and counting, children. They've faced obstacles and overcome them. And still the vision continues to grow.

"The vision that is not alive is not a vision," says Piet. "And for me, I don't even call it a vision. If I have a family, I have to care for them…What would you do for your kids? You want them to have the best education, you want them to have the best health care, you want them to have the best future plans, the morals—all that. So if you call that vision, it's fine. For me, it's just what you do for your kids."

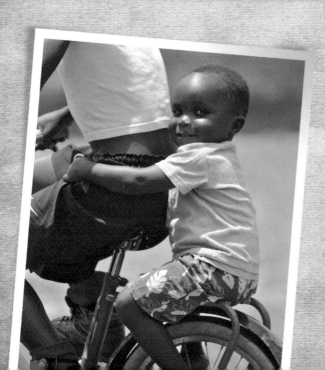

Springbank

Nestled between the 'men's breakfast' and the 'baby shower' notice in the bulletin is an announcement for this year's Mukono trip. Dates, number of spots available, where you can find the sign-up sheet and whom to talk to for more information is all listed there.

It could be easy to skim over this notice if you dropped by Springbank Community Church, located in the suburbs of Calgary, Alberta. But this small bulletin blurb signifies something important. It's a sign of Springbank's commitment to sending teams into the mission field.

This is a rich church in one of the wealthiest postal codes in Canada. When the church leadership began looking at ways to expand their missions focus, the financial aspect of partnering with a missions organization overseas was never a concern. Raising funds would be the easy part.

They chose to work with Noah's Ark Children's Home in Mukono, Uganda, an orphanage with more than 100 children and growing. When we interviewed Ana, the church's office

"You can see the love; it's just there in them."

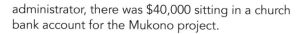

administrator, there was $40,000 sitting in a church bank account for the Mukono project.

"We've never asked for money for Mukono," Ana says. "People keep giving, so that's been pretty amazing."

What is harder, muses Ana, is for people who are used to just writing a cheque to instead give of their valuable time. The trips started off slow, with only six people from the church going on the second trip. But by the time Springbank was ready to send their third team, they maxed out on volunteers with 14 people signed up.

"It's been good," Ana reflects.

The church has now sent at least one missions team a year to Noah's Ark. It has helped the people at this church to step outside their comfort zone and take the time to connect with Noah's Ark and the work being done there.

Ana knows this partnership has been good for the congregants of Springbank.

"It's so easy to get lost in North American culture," says Ana. "We need a larger worldview."

She has become the point person for the Mukono project at her church. Ana loves it when she's able to travel to the children's home; she admires the work that founders Piet and Pita Buitendijk are doing in Mukono, Uganda.

"I don't understand how two people can love that many kids and still be able to accept more," she says. "You can see the love; it's just there in them."

An announcement in the bulletin might not seem like much. But it translates into both changed lives and changed hearts for orphans in Africa and the affluent in North America.

Nina

Nina is a woman after God's own heart. She seeks the lost, she comforts the afflicted, she blesses those around her with a peace that can only come from the Lord.

It's easy to love Christ when life has been good. When there is no trial, no persecution, you can thank God for all His blessings and live your life comfortably.

But Nina has not had a comfortable life.

She lives in a concrete building, up nine flights of stairs, dimly lit from grimy window panes. Unit #17. Here this 63-year-old widow lives alone in her sparsely-furnished apartment in the city of Nikopol, Ukraine.

Life started out hard for Nina. Growing up, Nina lacked a good relationship with her father. She was disobedient, and recalls one time when her dad grabbed her and shouted at her.

"After that, in my heart, I became very careless about him. I didn't have love towards my dad," she shares.

As a young woman, Nina was sexually abused. She became depressed and wanted to end her life. But she heard a voice in her head that said to not kill herself, and she listened.

As an adult, Nina came close to having an affair with a married man. It started off innocently. But it quickly grew more serious and he even told Nina he would leave his wife for her.

"I started to hope on this man, like I would have a life with him. But when he told his wife, she gave him an ultimatum and he changed his mind. It was very hard for me," she says. "But now I am so thankful to God that it never happened."

Like most little girls, Nina grew up dreaming of getting married, living in a nice house and starting a family. And eventually this is just what she did. But contrary to her hope that life would finally improve, it only got worse. Her husband was uncaring; he sidelined Nina and their children and left them craving love. Twice they divorced and got back together.

"He never cared for us, the family," she says.

Much emotion and a lot of history rests behind Nina's summary of this time in her life. She says simply, "Life was very bad."

She seeks the lost, she comforts the afflicted.

live, Nina began searching for something more. She remembered hearing the Lord's prayer as a child and began to search for what it meant. She ended up at an Orthodox church, the leading religion of Ukraine. She paid to baptize the children there but when she saw there was no change in the family, she grew more disheartened.

Meanwhile, Nina's superior at work began bringing in a preacher to read the Bible and teach. Nina attended the classes, and felt convicted. During this time, Nina's son fell gravely ill and she had no money for bribes to get doctors to help him, or for medication or proper food.

Her superior at work urged Nina to pray for her son's health. She got on her knees and started to pray.

"And then I found a joy in my heart," she shares. "After that, colour came. The sky was blue, the grass was green."

Nina's husband was involved in a life of crime; it became so dangerous they packed up their lives and fled to her parents' town in Russia to escape the criminal world. But he continued to drink, cheat on Nina and disregard their children.

The town they moved to was filled with gang activity and the local gangs would often take young men and drag them into that life. Nina feared their teenage son would be forcibly taken into a gang. So they moved again, this time to Nikopol, Ukraine. But her husband's bad habits followed them.

Nina's husband would often leave her but would always return. One day, Nina's husband left and never came back. While there is no evidence of his death, Nina is certainly a widow now.

But God can take even bad situations and turns them into good. As she faced the life she hadn't chosen to

Her son got better, and Nina grew stronger in her faith as she studied the Bible and prayed. Just three months after she repented, Nina was baptized.

With Nina's husband gone and her children grown up and working far away in Russia where the jobs are, Nina is very much alone. Living in Ukraine means paying a premium for heating, and Nina could not afford to have heat in her home during the long, cold winters. For months on end she faced freezing temperatures, sleeping in her coat and always, always feeling cold.

While she believed in Christ and put her trust in Him, it got to the point where Nina didn't think she could bear another winter of cold. Those thoughts of suicide she had as a young woman crept back into Nina's heart and began to take hold. For Nina, suicide was not an easy way out, but it was a warmer thought than braving the cold for months on end.

Then a miracle happened. Her pastor's wife, Nadia, approached her one Sunday and asked if she would like to have heat brought into her home.

"I had never shared my problems with anybody that I had this issue. But God revealed it to Nadia and Pastor John," Nina recalls.

No words could express her feelings at that moment.

"When I told her that heat would be installed in her home, she burst into tears," Nadia recalls. "She told me she had been thinking about death with the winter coming up and the stress of it being so cold. I told her, 'The Lord wants you to have a warm house now'."

A team from Canada had raised an abundance of funds for their upcoming missions trip to Ukraine and had gotten in touch with Nadia to see how the funds should be distributed. Nadia had felt for several years that Nina needed some help but had no finances to assist her.

Nina used to dread the cold of her home. Now each time she turns on her heat, she feels blessed that Christians from across the world would willingly help out a poor widow.

"To me, this was something impossible," she shares.

Nina sees God working in her heart, sprouting results in her life.

"I know God wants to make me complete," she says, gazing out her window at the grassy field in view. "See, there is a tree there. It has an old root—the trunk is very old. But every year, it brings very good fruit. It's actually very sweet."

She pauses, making sure the right tree has been identified. "God, through this tree, tells me just to trust Him and I am going to bear fruit."

Nina lives in poverty, that much is obvious. Yet she does not ask God for more. She prays, "Don't make me too poor so I steal; don't make me too wealthy because I know how I am and I would forget."

God has provided for her basic necessities in life. And out of her poverty, Nina gives to those less fortunate than her. She visits people in the hospital, knows ladies even poorer than her and cooks for them, taking money from her own pension to help.

Nina has sought forgiveness of those she wronged years ago and has restored her relationship with her father. She sees God working in all the situations through her life, and continues to bring Him praise through the good and the bad.

At a small table by the sunlit window Nina sits and shares her story with us, lovingly clutching her Bible as she speaks. She opens up her Bible, passages marked throughout its well-worn pages.

"I read and God reveals," Nina explains. "Even today, I was reading Isaiah 12 before you came. It says 'And that day you will say: Give thanks to the Lord, call on His name; make known among the nations what He has done, and proclaim that His name is exalted'."

She says that is what she wants to do, to use her life as a testimony to God's glory, to proclaim His deeds among the nations and to remind them that His name is great.

"Praise be to God," she concludes. "Praise be to God."

This tree serves Nina as a reminder to trust in God.

Garden project

In the poverty-stricken Siaya District of Kenya, there's a project underway that's changing the earth. The dirt is becoming rich in production and people are finding themselves in an unfamiliar but amazing situation: they have enough to eat.

For families like Mary and Bonfas, this is a most welcome change.

Mary says they used to have a garden, "but it became unproductive."

With 10 children to feed, making the few vegetables they could eke out of the soil stretch to feed the family was impossible. They had to go to the market to buy produce, which cost money the family simply didn't have. Their living situation was dire.

Then they heard about their pastor's flourishing garden. Pastor William had learned new techniques from another pastor who had gone through a training program and was now passing the knowledge on to others.

The program itself, funded jointly through Hillside Community Church in Coquitlam, B.C. and the Canadian International Development Agency (CIDA), paid for seven pastors to undergo training in proven farming methods. They learned techniques like digging down four feet into the soil to allow better water retention, using natural pesticide control and growing nursery beds. As instructors taught the methods to create and maintain an effective garden, trainees cultivated their own plots and began to see results.

Green and growing gardens are a rare sight in the district so people quickly took notice. Interest grew, and the first generation began training friends and neighbours. As word spreads, more and more people are learning how to beat the dry African land into submissive soil ready for fertile beds of kale, tomatoes, onions, cabbage, maize and other nutritious foods.

This is a huge accomplishment, considering the Siaya District is in a food deficit for eight months of the year and imports basic foods from other countries and districts in Kenya. More than 50 per cent of the district is unable to meet basic food requirements. But through this program, the initial teaching to seven pastors has translated into more than 120 people trained within the first few months alone.

For Mary and Bonfas, the training means they can now gather vegetables from their own garden to feed their sizeable family. And their story is echoed in other plots

Lillian (left) and Bonfas & Mary (centre) are reaping the results of training.

of land throughout the district. Trainee Lillian says the old methods of farming were unproductive. Now, she is growing enough to feed her family and gets upwards of 100 shillings when she brings produce to the market to sell. It's not much money in our eyes (roughly $1.20 CAD), but to Lillian's family, it makes a big difference.

These third generation farmers are evidence the program is working, as the message gets passed from one family to the next. Families are now digging themselves out of extreme poverty, eating nutritious food right from their own gardens and passing on valuable knowledge to those around them. It's a miracle to see harsh soil turned into fertile land, and that miracle is being replayed again and again in Siaya, Kenya today.

Pastor William's garden is a thriving example of what's possible with better farming methods.

Reaching a lost world

The high Peruvian mountains barricade us in, making an isolated village feel even more distant from the rest of the world. Rays of sun are punctuated with a cool breeze. Students in school uniforms play soccer in the field while adults visit nearby under the shade of wide-brimmed, felt hats.

Cutting across the landscape is a thin, brown ribbon, a road just wide enough for one sturdy vehicle to make its way up and up and up to the village of Percca, Peru. Here is where ATEK works. Across the valley is a glimmer of another village. ATEK works there too. And the unmarked, tiny settlements along the steep and treacherous dirt road leading to these villages, ATEK works in those places as well.

Like many countries, Peru's indigenous people are a minority group. The natives here are the Cusco-Quechua people; they have a different language and culture than the Spanish majority.

Problems are unfortunately all-too-common in these Quechua communities. Alcoholism is rampant, sexual abuse is prevalent, and farm production is poor. So people go hungry and, if crops are bad, extreme conditions for families aren't far behind. Students in school are taught to read and write in Spanish even though their native tongue is Quechua, leading to a lack of pride in their language and culture.

But through ATEK, things are turning around. ATEK is using education as an opportunity to transform communities. The organization formed after area pastors gathered to discuss the overwhelming problems facing the Quechua villages, and looked at ways they could help.

"We started from zero; we had nothing," says founding member Pastor Fredi, ATEK's director. "We started to walk forward and found that God was with us."

Their model is to send staff into communities to train leaders in areas such as literacy, spiritual leadership and marriage counselling. Those community members then teach their own people. Results have been astounding: men stop beating their wives, families start working together instead of against each other, children start treating their parents with respect, and parents start treating children as gifts from God instead of just labourers.

In this oral society, men and women are learning to read in Quechua so they can understand the Bible in their native language. As they dig into the Truth, they are transformed.

As this organization begins to work in one village, residents from neighbouring communities hear and beg them to come to their village too. And so the work keeps spreading and growing as non-Christians beg this Christian organization to help their community.

Antero Cruz Miranda is a church leader in Percca. He has seen lives transformed in his village.

"People have stopped drinking and stopped beating each other up," he remarks.

Antero and his wife took ATEK's marriage counselling training and learned how to improve their own marriage so they could help others. There were Christians in Percca before ATEK began working here but Antero says it was a challenge to grow in faith with no trained pastors, no ability to study the Bible, and no materials to learn more about Christianity. The literacy training ATEK conducted has changed that.

"When we learn how to read and write, then we can read [the Bible] and pass on understanding to others," Antero explains.

Albino Mamani took ATEK's literacy training so he could read the Bible in his own language. When his training was through, Albino noticed others had the same desire to read. But without access to a program such as ATEK's in their isolated villages, there was no way for them to learn.

Antero holds his daughter as he shares his story.

Pastor Fredi visits with Antero after bringing Bibles to Percca.

CUSCO QUECHUA BIBLE
(BROWN —)   QCR 052P
24 COPIES
BOOKS KEEP DRY
MADE IN KOREA

So Albino became a literacy facilitator and has worked at ATEK for more than four years. He has seen real transformation in people's lives as a result of the literacy training; it gives people a sense of power to be able to read and write in their own language.

To reach the dozens of communities where ATEK works, staff travel by motorbike over extremely bumpy, windy and steep roads, or they take severely overcrowded public transportation. Albino spends many days each month on the road and in countless villages helping his Quechua people. For Albino, it's all worth it.

"It's love for my brother that makes me stay here," he says. "I'm here because that's what the Lord asks of me."

Others at ATEK feel the same way. Pastor Eusebio Chuctaya is the co-ordinator of ATEK's Family Ministries, which includes leadership, stewardship and marriage. He trains leaders in marriage seminars, which focus on strengthening families. Even within church leadership, couples struggle with their marriage.

Eusebio sees real transformation in the couples that take the marriage seminars. He explains that in the first session, they often see men and women sit on opposite sides of the church. Simple steps like getting husbands and wives to sit together are challenges the trainers face before even getting into details of how to work on a marriage.

Pastor Eusebio teaches by lantern in the remote village of Percca.

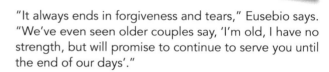

"People come to the seminars out of curiosity, wanting to know what the teaching is about and to judge how much the trainers really know," Eusebio says. "Others come because they realize they have problems."

But by the third and final workshop, the couples find promise of a new beginning.

"It always ends in forgiveness and tears," Eusebio says. "We've even seen older couples say, 'I'm old, I have no strength, but will promise to continue to serve you until the end of our days'."

And it's moments like these that make it all worthwhile for Eusebio.

ATEK works in small villages scattered in the mountains.

"We do it because we love God, we love our culture, we love our people," he says. "We travel a lot. But we are called by God to do this…And we understand we're not alone. We're part of the whole body."

The task of reaching the unreached and training will probably never be finished for ATEK. While the number of Christians are growing, ATEK can only reach a handful of villages at a time. There are thousands more Quechua going through similar problems in need of someone to come alongside and help. When asked how many unreached people there are left in the mountain areas surrounding Cusco, staff member

Tomas Puma answers with a heavy sigh: "Many…A lot of places need restoration or revival."

And so they continue. The men and women who work at ATEK have seen a picture of a world transformed, and they will continue to persevere and reach out and teach as long as God calls them.

"We pray that God opens the doors so we can continue forward," says Tomas. "There are so many unreached communities that need the Gospel."

Crossroads

The purpose is to be transformed and to allow God to pull him out of his comfort zone.

This is a story about a church. This is a story about a church that loves Jesus. This is a story about a church that loves Jesus and wants to be His hands and feet to the world.

This is a story about Crossroads Community Church in Chilliwack, B.C.

Pastor Rob loves his church, and loves its outlook on missions. He calls it a 'glocal' focus: global and local. He explains that each person, wherever he or she is placed in this life, is in a mission field of family, friends, coworkers, the barista at the coffee shop or the guys in the drop-in league. Rob says it's not about evangelism but about relationship-building, about sharing life together and about showing Christ's love through actions.

The global part of Crossroad's missions is seen as an extension to missional living at home. Crossroads partnered with Pastor Tomas in Mexico, also with an emphasis on relationship-building. Teams from the church made annual trips to work with Pastor Tomas as he ministers to the indigenous people of Mexico, the Tarahumara and Pima Indians.

While Rob acknowledges not everyone can go on a short-term missions trip, he has seen the dramatic changes that occur when people step outside their comfort zones and dedicate their time to the Lord.

Take Matthew, for instance. A younger guy who believed in God but is human and made some bad life choices. He signed up to go on a missions trip to Mexico and, while there, the team faced some challenging circumstances. In situations where only God could be the answer, God answered and Matthew found his faith renewed.

Then there's Rosie. Committed, passionate, all gung-ho about Crossroads and everything it represents. She went to Mexico and got scared out of her wits on a precarious "road" to the project site. It was so bad, she actually hopped out of the vehicle and asserted she would walk the rest of the way. She was, as Rob puts it, "scared spit-less."

It seemed that Rosie would never want to be involved in global missions again. She had one of the worst experiences Rob has ever seen or heard about from someone on a missions trip.

But as part of the leadership team, Rosie has been the one calling on Crossroads to stay connected to missions and is passionate about helping their partner in Mexico, even if it means travelling there again.

To have someone going from being so scared they don't think they'll survive to advocating a return trip—saying she'd go back in a heartbeat—shows significant heart-change to Rob. He sees people being renovated for Christ through experiences like these missions trips. It's in the going that for some people stretches them beyond what they would have otherwise experienced.

Rob doesn't particularly enjoy missions trips either. But he knows that's OK too, that the purpose is to be transformed and to allow God to pull him out of his comfort zone.

"I cry for the first half an hour of every trip," he honestly shares. "I love my family…I miss them when I'm gone."

But he always reaches a point where he is OK in the going because he knows what it does for his own heart and how it impacts the team members. He cares deeply for his church and as one of the ways to encourage them to expand, he goes with them on these journeys.

"It's good for your heart, your soul, your state of being."

And he loves how the transformation of hearts on a missions trip leads to transformed lives at home. For example, when the short-term missionary teams help to feed people in remote villages, they come back home and start looking for people who need food here.

"It causes us all to look for [the needs] here," Rob explains. "Missions is about where you are, about being who you are… You're a missionary every day."

"You're a missionary every day."

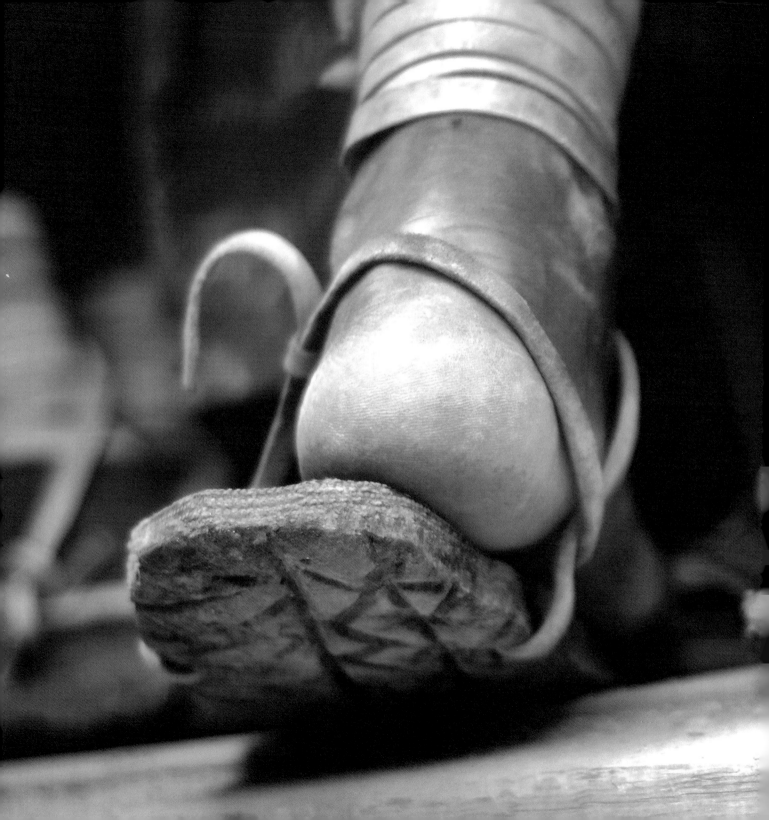

Domtila

This woman used to feel aching hunger. Now she fills her belly. This woman used to see her children and grandchildren starving. Now she sees them eat. This woman used to know despair. Now she knows hope.

This woman is Domtila. Here, in the village of Ndere, Pastor Samuel's garden has become a hands-on school as villagers learn better growing techniques. Domtila, Pastor Samuel's mother, tells us their neighbours couldn't believe the growth they witnessed when the garden started to sprout crops. Villagers were skeptical. Now they see the thriving garden and want to learn what Pastor Samuel's family has done to make such a difference in productivity levels.

"We've eaten so much, and not just eating. We have taken a lot of vegetables to the market," Domtila tells us through a translator.

Before Pastor Samuel took part in a training program made possible by a partnership between his church denomination and Hillside Church in Coquitlam, B.C., the produce from this garden was not enough to even feed the family.

Domtila stands in amazement at what has happened here. The garden is feeding families, it's opening the eyes of villagers to a new way of farming and it's allowing Pastor Samuel and his church family to tangibly show the love of Christ to the community. By providing free training in Ndere, villagers are seeing the church's love for them through actions, not just through words.

As she shares how the garden project has changed their lives, Domtila's gnarled bare feet form dusty swirls on the dry ground—a stark contrast to the nearby garden. With weathered hands, she gestures to their fenced-in plot: "Are you really seeing what is happening in the area? Are you really seeing that? [This program] has brought development into Ndere."

Domtila's garden is helping feed a village.

Amitha's smile
lights up the room.

The beach home

Within gated confines sits an unremarkable house, concrete walls painted a cheery yellow and a postage patch of grass out front. Through the barred windows you can see children laughing and playing.

Inside, Amitha Ranushki is one of the happiest looking kids. She is the youngest of three siblings, with a father too sick to work and a mother unable to make ends meet. But here at the Beach Children's Educational Centre in Moratuwa, Sri Lanka, Amitha is provided free early-education including a uniform, school supplies and a meal two times a week.

Amitha is one of 23 children attending the small preschool. The kids come from the slums of Moratuwa, a city on the outer reaches of the nation's capital. While you might observe these two to six-year-olds playing or singing inside, what you are really seeing is kids from impoverished families getting a chance at a future.

The children who attend the Beach Children's Educational Centre come from a destitute background. Families live in rows of makeshift squatter houses. The sandy pathways between homes lead to the water's edge, where mounds of garbage grow and stray dogs roam. Shacks smaller than a garden shed house anywhere from three to 10 people. Walls are made of scrap wood, cracks of light stream in through the holes, and cheap, ripped plastic lines the ceilings in an attempt to keep out the rain. Drug users and alcoholics live here. As a result, children are often swept into this lifestyle, teacher Lakmali Cooray tells us.

The community is isolated from the greater Moratuwa city by a clear geographical marker: it sits between the railroad tracks and the water, effectively cutting off the squatters from the rest of the world.

In a home no bigger than a single car garage, three-year-old student Upsaika lives with her parents and two siblings. Mother Madu Perera says her daughter would not be going to school if it were not for the free education offered at the centre.

The family is "helpless," Perera tells me. But here, her daughter is learning and that gives the whole family hope that their lives can someday change.

Perera says it's risky to live by the water; their home is mere metres from the high-tide line. But they have nowhere else to go, so they stay. Outside

Her daughter is learning and that gives the whole family hope that their lives can someday change.

her door, waves crash in a continuous reminder of the tsunami that struck swiftly and savagely only a few short years ago.

No one saw it coming. Hundreds of thousands bordering the Indian Ocean were caught off guard on December 26, 2004 when an undersea earthquake created a massive tsunami, with waves reportedly reaching as high as 30 metres. Nearly 230,000 people in 14 countries were killed. In the small island nation of Sri Lanka alone, more than 35,000 were confirmed dead and a staggering 516,000 displaced.

The Beach Children's Educational Centre was closed for the Christmas holidays when the tsunami hit. The building was completely destroyed. The wave also wiped out what little the families in this fishing community clung to, including household items, animals and the cobbled together walls they called their homes.

"Almost all the children lost everything," Lakmali recalls. "Because of the tsunami, the poor became more and more poor."

Waves of compassion from around the world followed one of the deadliest natural disasters in Earth's recorded history. In the community of Chilliwack, B.C. alone, more than $70,000 was raised. That money went to rebuild the Beach Children's Educational Centre. It was enough for the centre to relocate to another house further from the ocean's edge and open its doors to twice as many children. Funds also went to relief aid, a feeding program, fishing equipment and bicycles for fishermen and traders.

The students that attend the centre today are too young to remember the tsunami. Back at the bright and cheery building, Amitha, Upsaika and the 21 other students sing a song in English for guests from Canada. This centre is far enough away from the ocean that you cannot see or hear the waves. And for 23 families, their hope is that education will take these children to a new place, where they don't have to live next to the terrifying sea anymore.

Upsaika wouldn't be going to school if it wasn't for the beach home.

Proud teachers Lakmali & Rukshani (opposite).

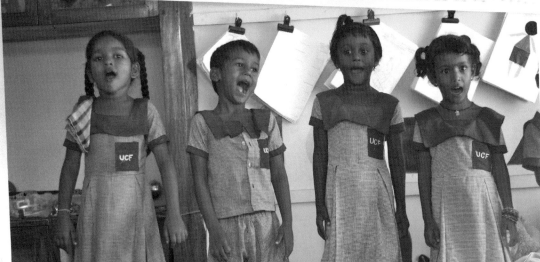

Under this mango tree, men and women share their stories of how they came to be at Haiti ARISE and how the community of Grand Goâve has been transformed.

Under the mango tree

In Haiti's Grand Goâve, a coastal community about two hours west of the capital city of Port-au-Prince, there sits a strip of land no more than four acres. The 15-foot walls surrounding this property encase a tropical green space complete with towering mango and palm trees.

There is a particular mango tree that sits in this property. This is where people often gather to swap stories, to talk faith, to impart wisdom. During the hot and humid days, the shaded boughs offer cool comfort and the vantage point is ideal to see all that goes on in the compound.

The dirt driveway cuts the mango grove from the guesthouse where short-term missions teams come to stay. To the left you can see the space where the technical and Bible school used to sit before the January 2010 earthquake and where a new building is now being constructed in its place. Behind the school foundation you can see the edge of the outdoor church where more than 450 people fill the pews and spill out into the grass, as hundreds of kids pile into one room for Sunday school.

Under this mango tree, men and women share their stories of how they came to be at Haiti ARISE and how the community of Grand Goâve has been transformed because of the faithful Christians serving here under the leadership of directors Marc and Lisa Honorat.

Stories like Nadia's are shared under this tree. Nadia was a frail, young woman when she came to Haiti ARISE for a free medical clinic run by a short-term missions team based in Cranbrook, B.C. She could barely walk and spent much of her life lying down because her heart didn't work right. Yet she somehow managed to make the estimated three-day journey from her home in the mountains to Grand Goâve.

The medical missions team, led by Dr. Bob Cutler, was able to cover the expenses for Nadia to have heart surgery. Before the surgery, it was estimated she only had six months to live. She is now a healthy and grateful 22-year-old.

"I thank God because I couldn't do anything before," she says quietly, glancing away as she talks.

Shy and sweet, Nadia spends her days at Haiti ARISE helping cook and be of assistance in any way she can. She's now able to go to school and is taking elementary-level classes. She praises God for saving her life, both spiritually and physically.

"Now she's enjoying life," says Marc. "It's a blessing for her, a blessing for us and a blessing to our community."

Haiti ARISE began a technical school in 2005 to train Haitians in practical job skills. Marc and Lisa saw the need for men and women to have practical training to

Nadia is grateful for missionaries like Dr. Bob. ↓

Wanachelow learned valuable skills at the technical school.

enable them to provide for their families. In a country of more than 80 per cent unemployment, having skills is of greater value than almost anything else.

"Our motto is not to give people fish. We want to teach them how to fish," explains Marc. "That's what Haiti ARISE is all about."

Wanachelow was one of the first students to take the carpentry program at the technical school. He loves that Haiti ARISE is helping raise up young people with valuable skills so they can help get themselves and their families out of the vicious cycle of poverty.

But more than that, Wanachelow sees the eternal benefits in the lives of those who come to Haiti ARISE, including his own.

"I see God working in my life. Before I was a Christian, I was different," he says. "Without having faith in God, I would be somewhere in a bad state."

Haiti ARISE also began an education fund, which has allowed them to send hundreds of children and young people to school, including Olrich.

Haiti ARISE paid for Olrich to become a tiler. After he finished his education, the Honorats helped Olrich even more. He plies his trade at Haiti ARISE and, in exchange, is paid in tools needed to start his own tiling business and have the means to pull himself out of a life of poverty.

As we listened to story after story under the mango tree, it sunk in how important ministries like this are. In North America, we have well-functioning levels of government. We have social assistance for people in financial need and food banks to feed hungry bellies. We have employment assistance programs, tuition aid and so many other opportunities. We have access to

Olrich plies his trade at Haiti ARISE.

hospitals and safe transit if we need to get to more specialized medical services.

In Grand Goâve, what do the people have? They have Marc and Lisa Honorat, and the team of people serving to help Haiti ARISE raise up godly men and women who will in turn help to turn the country around.

"We are here to help people," says Marc. "Transformed lives; it's helping the community and helping the country."

Everyone who sits under that mango tree has a story of how God has worked in their own lives and how Haiti ARISE is helping to transform a community and a country. God's workmanship is on display in the stories told under that mango tree in Grand Goâve, Haiti.

God's temple

Pastor Bazou has known Marc Honorat since he was 12 years old. That was when Marc was rescued from life as a restavec—a slave child—and was for the first time in his life given an opportunity to go to school.

Pastor Bazou came alongside the Honorats to help Haiti ARISE in any way he could. He sees amazing things happening on this holy ground.

"God is doing a great miracle here," Pastor Bazou says. "Especially here, where Haiti ARISE is located, it's a miracle place."

Leaning against the outer wall of the Haiti ARISE compound in the hot sun, Pastor Bazou points to the grassy compound grounds.

"Right there was a voodoo temple," Pastor Bazou shares. "Since Haiti ARISE came here and we bought this land, the voodoo temple changed into God's temple. For me, this is a big miracle. Through Haiti ARISE, the power of the devil is weakened; it's totally diminished here."

Dr. Bob

WRITTEN BY STEVE JOHNSON | PHOTOS BY BRIAN CLARKSON

Bob. A very common name in Canada, usually short for Robert. I think I have heard the name dozens of times. It follows the likes of Spongebob Square Pants, Bob the Builder, Billy Bob Thornton and Bobby Orr. Even when you put something in front of it to juice it up a little, like adding "Dr.," it doesn't jump off the page or roll off your tongue.

It is just "Dr. Bob."

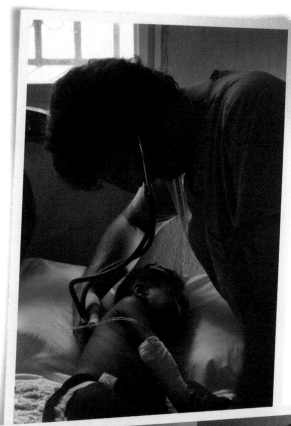

But it is not *just* "Dr. Bob" in Grande Goâve, Haiti. He is somewhat of a legend in these parts—my words, not his. He would say he loves to visit his Haitian brothers and sisters frequently and would help them out in any way he can. And help he does.

"Dr. Bob" is actually Robert Cutler, an MD from Cranbrook, B.C., who has been coming to Haiti in one way or another for more than nine years. In a quick calculation I would say he has treated over 10,000 Haitians in his time on this tiny island. The magnitude of this is astounding in a country where close to 60 per cent of children don't live to see their fifth birthday. But he doesn't keep track of the number of people he's seen or lives that he has touched in coming here. He doesn't get paid for this time and, in fact, is generous in making medical clinics operational.

His compensation for all of this is simply "Dr. Bob."

These words affectionaly come from the mouths of many: a little kid passing by on the path to the beach, an older gentleman coming to church and a lady collecting water for her family. They all know who he is, even if he doesn't remember all of them (because there are a lot). They are all people whose lives have been transformed by his work in this community.

In Haiti "Dr. Bob" signifies a life that has been changed. And that is worth more than anything in the world.

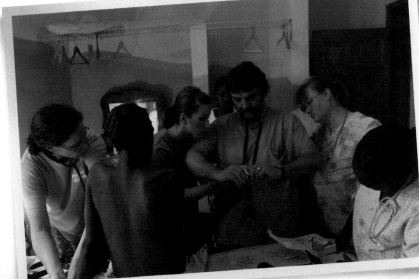

Roperta

Life in North America is about having it your way. Company slogans promise everything you want and more. You can choose the career, the lifestyle, the type of cream in your coffee—it's personal choice all the way.

So it might be hard to put yourself in the shoes of Roperta. Actually, she doesn't wear shoes; she wears sandals made from recycled tires. Most likely, it's her only pair.

Roperta lives in a tiny village called Perrca, high in the mountains of Peru. We're in this village with ATEK, a Christian organization helping Cusco-Quechua families, churches and communities grow stronger. The Quechua are the native residents of Peru.

Roperta is only 24 years old. In North America at that age, you might be married or paying off student loans, starting a career or still figuring out exactly what you want to do with your life.

At 24 and living in a small Quechua village, Roperta is a widow and a single mom. Her three-year-old son, Elvis, is growing up without a father, and Roperta is growing old quickly without a husband. She doesn't have much chance to get out of her tiny village and get an education. These choices do not exist here.

We meet Roperta to hear her story of transformation, one we're assured should be retold. Words are precious here. Roperta's Quechua language is complex and nothing like the national Spanish language. There are very few people who speak Quechua, Spanish and English. And unfortunately at ATEK, there is no single person who competently speaks all three languages.

So, if you want to talk to Roperta, you must first find a translator who speaks English and Spanish. Then you find a translator who speaks Spanish and Quechua. As each question is translated two times over, Roperta sits patiently on a wooden chair in front of the elementary school. Curious children surround the small circle of adults working to understand each other. After all, it's not often visitors come to this village, which takes approximately eight hours to drive to even though it's only 190 kilometres away from the modern city of Cusco, where ATEK is based.

I ask her to tell us her story, and while the translated words don't say much, they speak volumes.

"I've had a tragic life," Roperta says.

Her young husband died in an accident. To cope with the tragedy, Roperta began drinking, too-common a problem in these parts. Her life was on a downward spiral. But then Roperta heard about God from a man named Eriberto. He told her his own story of salvation and how Jesus could turn her life around.

"He spoke to my heart," Roperta says.

The next time there was an evangelism meeting, she went and gave her life to God. Becoming a Christian transformed her.

"I became free. I've been freed from the problems I had," she declares.

She now has joy, hope and freedom from her addictions and release from the problems of her past. She is serving in her community and has taken on the role of Sunday School teacher.

Like so many other things that we try to compare to what we understand, the role of Sunday School teacher does not match our North American construct. In these Quechua villages, ATEK trains Sunday School teachers, and for good reason.

"In the Quechua society, there is a belief that children aren't as important, that they don't belong in church," explains Yoni, the Sunday School trainer at ATEK. "That if you teach them about God, they're not going to learn."

Yoni, a Quechua woman herself, works to address those misconceptions, to show adults that children are a valued part of any church body and are able to learn about Jesus from a young age. Even Quechua Christians often do not understand that Jesus encouraged children to learn, for many cannot read the Bible in their own language.

"So the first workshop is simply teaching them that kids are important," Yoni explains.

Even for those who agree that children should be in church, ATEK has found many adults don't understand what it means to run a children's program.

"They've never seen how this works. They've never seen Sunday School or children's camp," says Yoni. "So how are they ever going to teach if they've never seen it happen?"

The third issue, and a big hurdle, is that even when they are able to convince adults why Sunday School is important and what happens there, they still face the obstacle of confidence.

"A lot of adults look at themselves and think they're not capable of teaching," Yoni says. "Many hardly even have a secondary eduction. They don't feel capable of being able to teach, so they're not stepping up to do it."

After another person from her village took the Sunday School training, Roperta knew that was what she wanted to do. She wants to teach children about Christ, to learn the Word of God and to tell them about the Christian life.

"We don't live forever, tomorrow we could die. It's important then to live in the faith," she says.

Roperta's prayer for Percca is to see everyone here turn to Christ.

It's been a pivotal shift for this community to see how Roperta changed. Parents took notice of how different she is and now want to send their children to Sunday School to learn about this new way of living. Roperta says others are curious about her transformation and often ask her about it. She has become, as the translator tells me, "a living testimony."

Roperta has become a living testimony.

10 Shillings

Wilfreda's weathered face reveals a life of hardship. She's a wisp of a woman with bones visible through her arms. Tufts of grey hair hide under a scarf most days, a wide-brimmed hat on Sundays. Her clothes are tattered and threadbare. Dust covers her dark cocoa-coloured skin and spreads thickly around her bare feet.

Wilfreda lives in a tiny mud hut in a small Kenyan village in the district of Boro. This is one of the poorest districts in Kenya, and that's saying a lot. There are no jobs, no food, no social services and no way for people like Wilfreda to make an income. She's not just poor; she's living in extreme poverty.

She has no financial security, no food security, no physical security. But she has found security in something that cannot be destroyed or taken away; she trusts her very life to the Lord.

Wilfreda arrives at church every week with a huge smile and welcoming hands, dressed in her Sunday best. The tin-roofed church is full of mostly widows and orphans. Some have probably not had anything to eat for breakfast; three meals a day is unheard of in Boro.

Pastor Michael's flock is a poor one. Yet they bring a joyful spirit to church as they arrive, greeting visitors and hugging each other.

They come to worship, and it is a sweet sound. Out of the congregation, one lone woman begins to sing praise to God. The rest repeat after her, moving and clapping their worship. As one song ends, another begins and so it goes, song after song.

There is such a presence of God in this place, and the humble surroundings make it all the more evident that God seeks after our hearts alone. Wilfreda sings out to her Saviour, giving Him her praise.

After the pastor's message comes time for the offering. A large basket is placed on a table at the front. One by

Worshipping in her Sunday best. ➘

one people make their way forward. They give small amounts—5, 10 or 20 shillings at the most—releasing their grip and dropping their meagre offerings into the handwoven basket with a clink.

Wilfreda is among them. She gives maybe 10 shillings— mere pennies in our eyes. But the sacrifice is huge. Seeing where she comes from, what she faces, the life she lives, it's obvious she doesn't have an 'extra' 10 shillings to drop in the basket.

Wilfreda gave a handful of change. But it was so much more than that. To see her give her offering to Christ was humbling. No sacrifice I can think of was greater than Wilfreda's 10 shillings that day.

She gives maybe
10 shillings—
mere pennies in
our eyes. But the
sacrifice is huge.

The Copper Canyon surrounds or suffocates, depending on your mindset.

Tarahumara

It's menacing and breathtaking. Up close, swaths of dusty rocks crowd shrubs, boulders and trees. But from far back, it's lush. Ribbons of rock course through the growing foliage, like blood veins on ancient hands.

The Copper Canyon in Mexico surrounds or suffocates, depending on your mindset. Its walls of brown and green rise up like sentinels, guarding the people and their culture within. It affects every aspect of life for its inhabitants. Homes are found in caves along the steep canyon edges or built on patches of chiseled earth. Everything is on a slope: pathways, buildings, children's play. What gardens exist have been etched from the inclines. And food is scarce when the inhospitable soil churns out more rocks than harvest. Many here have died of starvation. And some say the government has been slow to respond.

The canyon was a hiding place for the Tarahumara Indians. That was a good thing when this indigenous group first fled here to escape slavery at the hands of Spanish conquistadors more than 400 years ago. But now this source of refuge has become a trap. These people fear the outside world and have been left behind, caught in a life of subsistence.

The Tarahumara distrust outsiders, and even with each other their socializing is scarce. Small clusters of families live scattered throughout the canyon, preferring isolation over community. They are disconnected. Separated by choice, by custom and by the composition of the canyon.

There are thousands of Tarahumara living without education, without food, without the resources to be able to better their lives.

But in the tiny canyon village of Guacaivo, things are looking up.

Guacaivo is a world within a world, barricaded from civilization by the canyon walls. This world belongs to men like Alfredo Ramirez.

Alfredo first heard of God through Pastor Tomas. The travelling pastor ventured to the canyon after hearing that an entire population in Mexico was suffering and dying of starvation.

Groups of brightly dressed Tarahumara appear out of the rocky landscape. ↙

"We're not talking about a natural suffering," Pastor Tomas says of the Tarahumara. "We're talking about a spiritual heritage. This is an ancient tribe that has been attacked by all kinds of demons. They have always lived with fear and superstition."

Pastor Tomas began helping as many in the hard-to-reach areas of the Copper Canyon as he could. He came to Alfredo's village of Guacaivo after someone told him there were many old people in this village who were dying.

Pastor Tomas and his team assessed the needs and ended up bringing in a missions team of doctors. Since then, the Tarahumara Ministry team has been coming back to Guacaivo on a regular basis, bringing supplies such as food and clothing, and sharing the love of Christ.

"Before he arrived to this place, many of us didn't eat much," Alfredo shares. "They came to talk about God. And they wanted to help us, they wanted to help the people in the area."

On distribution day in Guacaivo, groups of brightly dressed Tarahumara women and cowboy-styled men

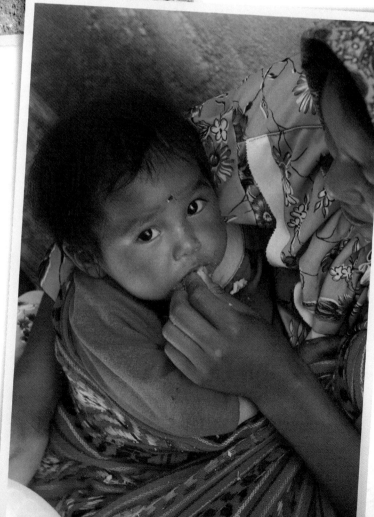

begin to appear out of rocks across the deep valley and along the steep mountainside.

They make quick work of the switchbacks, traversing back and forth until they reach the roadside and then downhill to Guacaivo. Provisions can include flour, sugar, tins of meat, fabric and toys. When Pastor Tomas and his team can, they also bring bags of clothing. Most Tarahumara have a fear of strangers. But because they need the food so badly, they come.

As Pastor Tomas' team started working in places like Guacaivo, they saw a need for more than just immediate relief assistance. While the food and clothing distributions help to connect and reach out to the people, that is a stopgap measure. In 2009, the Tarahumara ministry opened a boarding school in Guacaivo to provide Tarahumara children with an education. It's giving kids a chance at a future they might not otherwise have.

Alfredo is happy the boarding school opened in his community.

"I see God working in a very special way. God has blessed this place," he remarks.

Just looking at what has been accomplished in Guacaivo over the last few years, Alfredo knows it was divine intervention.

"I see God in Pastor Tomas."

Alfredo and Victoria's four children go to school in Guacaivo now. Before that, they hiked in and out of the Copper Canyon every day. It was a perilous journey that took several hours, travelling narrow rocky paths to descend to the bottom of the canyon, across a raging river in a cable-hung basket and up the other side.

And community is forming within Guacaivo in a way it didn't exist before. The Christians here gather every Sunday to read the Bible, praise God together and encourage each other in their faith.

Alfredo was part of a world disconnected from our

own. Pastor Tomas and the Tarahumara Ministry have helped to open a door into this hidden world. Alfredo and his children have opportunities to work, to grow, to thrive. Missions teams from North America come to Alfredo's world now, and share encouragement and testimony. And with Alfredo's faith, his whole worldview has shifted. No longer is the Copper Canyon Alfredo's refuge: God is.

Alfredo wears a new hat atop his own, a gift from Pastor Tomas.

Coquitlam Alliance Church, Coquitlam, B.C.

This church has been heavily involved in the remote village of Guacaivo, Mexico for more than 8 years.

Mary

The first time Mary grasped how much stuff people had was when she started cleaning houses for a living. What might be considered normal by North American standards was overwhelming compared to Mary's home country of Ukraine.

"It was just insane," Mary says.

She got the idea to start gathering clothes—something we have plenty of—and sending them to Ukraine.

Knowing the desperate need there for such simple things as shoes and shirts, Mary and her husband Chad would collect clothes and save up money to ship a box. They sent the boxes to her sister working as a missionary on the opposite side of Ukraine from where she grew up.

Nadia and her husband, John, live and serve in Nikopol, Ukraine, ministering to the poor, the widowed, the orphaned and the hungry. There is a great deal of poverty in this country, and there is little in terms of support systems for those in need. The boxes Mary started to send helped John and Nadia reach out to people in need in and around Nikopol.

"I just felt like there was something more I should be doing. And that's when it hit me: I could make perogies and have people donate and all the money that I raise will go for widows and orphans in Ukraine," explains Mary.

She and some Mennonite women in B.C.'s Fraser Valley began cooking up perogies as a fundraiser. The first fundraiser dinner had 25 seniors in attendance and they raised $750.

"They prayed that would be the smallest cheque for this [type of fundraiser]," says Mary.

And it was. More than $100,000 has been raised since that first dinner. The Mennonite community has embraced this project, helping Mary to make hundreds of thousands of perogies, ship boxes and travel to Ukraine to serve with John and Nadia on short-term missions trips. Now, they send shipping containers full of clothes. And often, the people who have packed the clothes on this continent are the ones unpacking and distributing them on the other side of the world.

The money raised goes to helping widows and orphans in Ukraine, providing clothing, food and other basic necessities. It has covered hospital bills, helped finish houses, renovated churches and has provided for one specific orphanage a great deal. It's a way for Nadia and John to reach out

"If I didn't do it, I believe God would look after orphans and widows just as much as He's looking after them now and I would be the one who would miss out on the blessing."

Mary ministers to widows in the village of Shishkano, Ukraine.

Packing care bags with a team in Ukraine.

to people in a practical way, to show God's love in the community as well as in the church, and to provide real help to people who need it. And it's making a difference in people's lives, physically and spiritually.

"To have somebody who would actually care for you and who would think you are worth something—that you are not a burden—that's huge," Mary says.

Many churches have been planted through this ministry, many have come to know Jesus as their Saviour, many have been clothed, fed and practically cared for. Short-term missions teams have travelled to Nikopol to see the work in progress, to help unpack boxes they packed in Canada and distribute clothing to people who need it more than we can imagine.

"We have so much resources here—way more than what we need—and I think it's good if we are willing to share. And God gives us an opportunity," says Mary.

But for Mary, this impressive work is simply what she was called to do.

"It's just what I'm supposed to do. If I didn't do it, I believe God would look after orphans and widows just as much as He's looking after them now and I would be the one who would miss out on the blessing of not being a part of it. All of us have something to do. Some people, they are good with making a lot of money and they give through that and that's what they are good at. Other people like me, I'm making perogies and God is blessing that."

We got to witness several clothing distributions done by the Fraser Valley team while in Ukraine. We hosted a church banquet where we gave away clothes. As one woman browsed, she began to cry. She grabbed my arm, pulled me close and told me she had been wearing the same skirt for the last 20 years. This 72-year old widow had found another skirt and was overjoyed.

Mukumu Children's Home

When Grace looked around her community, all she could see was desperation.

There were scores of children in Kakamega, orphaned because of AIDS and poverty. They were living on the streets, or alone in their family homes with no protection. Children were being abused, victimized, raped. Someone needed to do something.

Grace is a retired teacher. She's not rich. Her home is a mere 850 square feet. But she has a roof and four walls on her own property. She knew God was calling her to do something to help.

So, on little more than faith and few funds, Grace opened the Mukumu Children's Home.

The orphanage now houses more than 30 children, with boys sharing one room and girls sharing another.

"We give them parental love, shelter and we take them to school," explains Grace.

Grace has a special concern for the devastating effects HIV and AIDS has played in the community. She says the superstitious Kenyan people believe children must be bad luck if their parents have died. Extended families often banish the child because they fear he or she will bring bad luck into another home.

"God called me to this project of taking care of the children," Grace shares.

She wants the community to see that children are innocent, that they are not responsible for their parent's deaths.

After five years of running the orphanage, Grace has seen the children grow and become healthier and, more than anything, act like kids again.

Yes, they are overcrowded. Yes, many days Grace isn't sure where the next meal might come from. But the children are safe and that's the most important thing.

"They have grown. They have a sense of belonging," she says.

But opening the home is not the end of this story. Grace would often see neighbouring children hover near the orphanage fence, looking longingly at the meagre portions of food Grace was able to provide her kids. They were hungry. They came from families unable to care for their basic necessities or send them to school.

So Grace started a school too.

"There needs to be change here. And I thought if I want to see change, I need to make change," she says simply of the undertaking.

There are approximately 90 children attending the elementary school. Grace says for many of the students, the cup of porridge she feeds them each day is probably the only thing they will eat.

"There is lots of starvation in this area; there is no food," she explains. "So when I bring them here, they learn a bit, then I give them a cup of porridge, then they sing and we play together. We have a short prayer in English, then they go to their village...You can see they are happy."

She would love to do more, but for now this is what she can do. She has opened her home, taken in more than two dozen orphans and is feeding and providing education for a small army of children from the community.

For Grace, it has all been worth it when she sees the transformation not only in the lives of the children she cares for, but in her own heart as well.

"I don't know what would have happened to me if I didn't (start this home)," says Grace. "There was a lot of change in me."

Kids line up to wash before eating.

Nola

There might not be a people more defined by their surroundings than in the American South. When you meet Nola, she seems the epitome of a Southern belle. She holds herself with dignity and talks with a distinctive sweet, slow drawl. She was born in Mississippi and lives in Louisiana—places that conjure up a thousand impressions, the words saturated with images of crocodiles and Cajun cooking, with hot, sticky weather and a slow pace of life.

But Nola's geography is not what defines her.

She was born a month before the Great Depression began. She's lived through World War II, the U.S. prosperity years, the Berlin Wall, the Gulf War, 9/11 and the war on terrorism. She was 39 years old when the first man ever stepped on the moon. In her lifetime, Bandaids and Polaroid cameras, bikinis and Gore-tex have all been invented. She was born on September 7, 1929. She could sit back, relax and take life as it comes these days.

But that's not Nola. She doesn't let her age constrain or define her.

Nola happily married her high school sweetheart Nolan. They had five children, a darling house and a bright future. But happily ever after never came.

Tragedy struck the family on June 16, 1974. Father's Day. She remembers it like it was yesterday. The whole family had breakfast together before heading off to a relative's wedding reception. The band started playing and Nolan asked their oldest daughter Shirley to dance. Suddenly he fell backwards on the floor. Heart attack. He died instantly.

"It was a horrible scene," she recalls. "We had to pick up the pieces of our lives; it was such a shock."

Coping with the sudden loss of her husband, Nola fell into grief. More than 35 years later, she still misses him.

Being a widow is certainly a large part of who Nola is; she still talks wistfully about her husband and the years they got to spend together.

Yet Nola doesn't even let her grief define her. And she's had more of that than any one person should bear.

The term 'Mom' encompasses so much of a woman's life: her passions, her prayers, her tears and time. Nola raised five children and she's proud of her role as a mother. As her kids grew up, not one ever came home from school to an empty house. She was happy to always be there for them.

Nola's second youngest child Tim died in October, 2001, from heart trouble. He was only 42 years old. It wasn't a big surprise, but that doesn't make the loss any easier.

Nola's oldest son Nick married and had two little girls. After his dad died, Nick, who had a rocky marriage anyway, began drinking. Nick lost his job, got a divorce, ended up hitting someone so hard he killed him and landed in jail. But he sobered up in prison, found Jesus and a good woman to love. He lived 13 years a happily married man.

"I prayed for 20 years that before I died, I could see Nick happy with a home, not drinking and all. And you know what? It happened," she utters, crying. "Prayers do not go unanswered."

Nick had survived throat cancer. They'd told him he might not survive, but Nola says by the grace of God, he lived through it. Then one day—a Monday afternoon—he was helping his stepson paint. He was at the bottom of the ladder and fell backwards. He'd had an aneurism of the heart and became unconscious.

"They took him to the hospital, but he never regained consciousness," Nola says. "They had to pull the plug, because he would've been a vegetable."

Then there was Kevin, Nola's youngest. "My baby," she whispers as she points to his picture.

After a liver transplant, Kevin had a new lease on life. But after five years, his liver failed and his quality of life took a drastic turn for the worse. He fought to live, and they prayed and hoped above all hopes he would survive. Kevin died at age 48.

"It's been tough since I lost him…So I just kept working and trying to make myself busy, busy, busy. I would not let 'em get the best of me," she says with defiance.

She's still very sad her boys are gone. "I miss them," she puts simply. But she's learning to be happy. And now when she looks at their pictures, she can do so without crying. She grasps a picture frame of her family and says she did ask God why He let her survive, to live through all of this hurt. But she has come to understand that while she might never have that answer, she had time with them and that's what's important.

"I thank God He let me have them for as many years [as I did]."

Motherhood is a strong source of identity, especially for someone who invested as much in motherhood as Nola did. But if Nola's children provided the meaning for her life, she might not even be alive right now, overwhelmed by the tragedy. It's an understatement to say Nola misses her sons. But Nola lives on. She's not just satisfied with her lot in life; she's content.

Nola's children do not define her.

Nola still lives in the same clapboard house she and her husband bought 60 years ago. She has maintained it, renovated it, even sewn all the curtains. Here, she raised her children, built up a flourishing garden, has friends over for tea. Here also is where two major hurricanes have hit. Hurricane Camille was the "big one" around these parts, the one that people talked about. That was in 1967. Camille stole Nola's roof but left the rest of the house intact.

Then on August 29, 2005, Hurricane Katrina attacked the South. While most people heard about the devastation in New Orleans, it was actually Nola's community of Bay St. Louis and Waveland, Mississippi that was ground zero.

"When Katrina hit, it took everything we had," she recalls. "It was like a Third World country, like you see

people overseas starving in the street with nothing… There was people looting, stealing everybody's stuff. Oh it was horrible. Horrible y'all."

She had escaped the storm along with 18 other relatives to her grandson's home outside the affected area. When she came back, she couldn't believe her house was still standing. Water had flooded the town; everything inside was wet and covered in mud but the house stood firm.

"See this storm was kinda peculiar," she comments. "You can go 'round town and you see positively nothing left to a house. And then you come down this street and you see every house still standing."

The towns of Waveland and Bay St. Louis lost about half their population as people moved away after the storm, including at least half of Nola's neighbours. She says it will never be the same here.

"We are struggling to come back."

Yet she says, "Everybody here is blessed with what happened to us after Katrina."

Blessed? She explains it's because of the storm that she's met so many wonderful people. She has a scrapbook of letters, notes, photos and cards from volunteers that worked on her home. She says without the volunteers, even with her insurance money, she would never have been able to move back.

"We were so grateful, because you don't really believe that there's that many kind people in this world," she says of all the volunteers who came to rebuild her floor, remove and replace her mouldy cabinets, paint, build a deck, repair her garage, restore her belongings, and feed and clothe her. Most of all, she was grateful for all the encouragement and friendship she found in the scores of volunteers who flooded Mississippi after Hurricane Katrina.

However, in spite of the massive change this storm brought to Mississippi and to Nola's life, having a Category 5 hurricane rip through her home and

destroy her community has not been the defining moment in her life.

Truthfully, the hurricane was just one in a lifetime of storms. Nola has weathered much. And through it all, she has kept God the front and centre of her focus.

"Through all my grief, losing my sons and husband and the storm, I really believe God doesn't give us more than we can take," she states.

After the storm, Nola asked volunteers to install a large wooden cross in her front yard. She felt called by God to put up this holy symbol, as a 'God site' in the town.

"Many a people, volunteers, have come here wanting to know the story of this cross," Nola says. "And they have gathered in my front yard and prayed and gone back home and told people about the cross."

She sees blessings that come to those who wait on the Lord. While she has endured more hurt than most, Nola is filled with a joy in the Lord that is her strength.

"There's always a joy that comes back in your sadness. No matter how bad things get, there comes a time you sit down and think—for every sorrow there is a joy."

Certainly, there are many definitions to explain who Nola Kingston is. She's a wife and mother, a Southern belle, a hurricane survivor, a widow, a senior citizen. But through it all, God has been her strength, her pillar, her focus. She's a Christian, and that is what defines Nola.

Ben

Ben Zimmer and his two brothers grew up in the Canadian Prairies under the watchful gaze of strong Christian parents.

Ben had been in and out of the hospital as a child because of a cleft palate and didn't have many friends growing up. Just as he began making friends and feeling more comfortable with himself, the family moved to a small town about 30 minutes outside Edmonton, Alberta called Stony Plain.

He had become a Christian when he was four years old. But when the family moved, Ben's faith spiralled.

"That was definitely a low point for me. I was quite depressed and suicidal at points," he says. "I was angry at God for making me this way."

Ben's older brother and two friends had gone on a Teen Missions International trip to Greece, and when Ben became a teenager he decided to do a similar trip. But as the time drew closer, he had doubts whether he wanted to go and serve a God he was angry at. It was at that time he went to a Christian conference called Break Forth. There, he clearly heard God speak to him and tell him to go to Peru.

So in the summer of 2005, Ben spent five weeks in Pulcallpa, Peru on a missions trip.

"That's when I really started to fall in love with Peru and the culture and the language," Ben recalls.

One missions trip was not enough; Ben wanted to do more.

He finished high school and did a year of Bible school. Then he took a six-month discipleship training program called YWAM, which included three months overseas. Based out of Budapest, Hungary, Ben did outreach work in Bulgaria, Romania, Greece and Armania.

Near the end of his time with YWAM, Ben began praying about what to do next and felt called to return to Peru. It was just after that when Ben found out his church back in Stony Plain—Beach Corner Evangelical Free Church—had decided to get involved in missions in Peru. The day after he returned home from Europe, the church was doing a polar bear swim to raise money for the first missions trip. He was happy to see the growing enthusiasm in his church over the same country he himself had become so passionate about.

Ben was asked if he would like to go and he jumped right on board. The team went in July 2008 to Cusco, Peru to work with a group called ATEK.

ATEK is an interdenominational Christian organization that works with the Quechua-speaking people in the region surrounding Cusco. ATEK's vision is to build up healthy Quechua families, contributing to strong Quechua churches, contributing to unified and organized Quechua communities. Instead of international missionaries running the organization, ATEK is run by nationals who train community leaders to teach their own people. ATEK ministry fields include literacy, marriage counselling, pastoral and Sunday School teacher training, discipleship and other programs as finances and time allow.

"This is Quechua people from the villages getting training, going back out there—understanding the culture perfectly, the language perfectly—and bringing the Gospel in understandable cultural ways," Ben explains. "I was just blown away by their vision."

After he went home, Ben stayed in contact with ATEK and began discussing how he could come help this organization on a longer-term basis.

"I asked if they had need for a 'gringo' (white person) who doesn't speak Spanish to come down and help," he recalls with a laugh.

On the church's next trip to Cusco, Ben went again. But this time, he didn't leave. Ben committed two years to live and work with the Quechua people as they reach out to their own.

Ben's work allows the Quechua to hear the gospel.

Literacy levels are low in most villages and the written Cusco-Quechua language is challenging. So while the Bible has been translated into the Cusco-Quechua language, it doesn't mean it's being widely read. Another challenge ATEK has faced when it comes to spreading the Gospel is the lack of pastors. Many of the little villages have churches but no pastors to help the people understand Christianity more.

"They need pastors. But they also need the Word of God," says Ben. "It's been said that the Quechua Church is miles and miles wide, but an inch deep."

So Ben's task was to start up a program called 'Faith by Hearing'. With the use of digital players called Proclaimers, Ben is working to get the Gospel to unreached Quechua people. The Proclaimer has transformed the way the Gospel is being spread since literacy is no longer a barrier.

The foundation of this program is Romans 10:17: "Consequently, faith comes from hearing the message, and the message is heard through the Word of Christ." With the Proclaimers, people are learning and their faith is growing. In the first two months of Ben's ministry, two people had already become Christians through 'Faith By Hearing'.

"It's been really exciting to see what God is doing," Ben says. "People are so hungry for the Word of God."

Ben shares the story of going to one village to talk about the Proclaimer and see if the people wanted him to come back and have a training session for the device. When one man found out the Proclaimer is an audio Bible, he responded enthusiastically, "We want that, come back soon!"

Ben goes wherever ATEK is working. So if they go into far-off villages on motorbikes, Ben goes. If they go by bumpy vehicle on roads cut out from the mountainside, Ben goes. He travels from ATEK's Cusco base often: to train, to check up on the equipment and ensure it's being used correctly and to provide technical support as needed.

He sleeps on church floors and houses with guinea pigs and chickens running around. And he's eaten more guinea pig than he'd care to admit.

Ben's learned a lot during his time in Peru. It's been a challenge relying on God for everything from learning the language to finding community in a new country.

"We were never meant to do the Christian walk alone," he says. Having felt the isolation of living, working and worshiping in a different language, Ben has found a deeper appreciation for the work he's doing, for the Christian brothers and sisters working alongside him and for his trust in a God who never lets him down.

Back in Stony Plain, Ben has become a tangible link between Beach Corner and ATEK. The church members have really taken ownership over the partnership and project, in large part because one of their own is serving with ATEK. Ben sends back regular updates and he has even had live web chats with the congregation during Sunday service.

Reflecting on this journey, Ben says before God spoke to him at that pivotal conference where he was told to go to Peru, he hadn't felt right with God and wasn't sure why he should go serve.

"From that point on, I started changing my view of how He created me, and it really opened my eyes to see what the devil wanted—to shut my mouth, to shut me up with this birth defect in my mouth," Ben shares. "But God wanted to use my broken mouth to bring the Gospel to many different countries. He's done that already all throughout Europe and here in Peru. From that point on when I started actually living my faith, I was freed from a lot of bondage."

A people in Peru are being changed through the Gospel because of one man's willingness to go serve. A small Prairie town is being connected in tangible ways to a ministry a world away. And one young man's life has been dramatically altered because he listened and obeyed.

Nalwadda Rose

In a country where education is a luxury, not a right, Nalwadda Rose is one of the lucky ones.

School in Uganda costs money that most families cannot spare, and Nalwadda's family was no different. They could barely make ends meet, much less afford an education for their eldest of four children. Nalwadda's future path seemed set: to hopefully survive, grow up, get married and struggle to support her own family with no education and little opportunity.

Her story continues much like others in Africa. First her father died of AIDS, followed by her mother. Then her grandmother passed away, leaving Nalwadda to look after her three siblings on her own. She was 12, living in a shack, full of despair and empty of hope.

Seven kilometres up the road sits Noah's Ark Children's Home. This Christian-based organization cares for more than 130 children, most of whom came in as orphaned babies or toddlers.

Founders Piet and Pita Butendijk also built a school on the Noah's Ark grounds to ensure the children are well educated.

Noah's Ark opened the school doors to the surrounding community, seeking out the poorest of the poor and offering free education. And that's how Nalwadda Rose was found. In an area full of impoverished children, her story struck a chord and she was invited to come learn at the New Horizon Nursery & Primary School.

"When we went there, we really felt pity on that girl," Headmaster Sam Nsereko says. "We said maybe we can bring her to school, give her an opportunity. She can get a chance of getting a good job and taking care of those other children."

Nalwadda is now 14 and in her second year at school. It's a one-hour walk on a hot and dusty dirt road. But she is very grateful for the opportunity and says she doesn't mind the walk.

"I like school, I like to study," this shy teenager says, adding she would like to become a teacher some day.

Her aunt has now moved in, along with her own three children, to help raise the kids while Nalwadda goes to school. Through Noah's Ark, a total of four children in this extended family are now receiving free education.

Nalwadda is one of about 200 students that come from the community. An additional 80 students live at Noah's Ark. Sam says it's shocking to see the circumstances in which the community kids live, and cites Nalwadda's case as unfortunately not rare.

"Most of the kids here are being raised by grandparents as their parents have died of AIDS," Sam says. All are living in extreme poverty, and the only meals most of the community students eat are the breakfast and lunch served at school.

After graduating, students can attend vocational school on the grounds as well. It provides practical training to ensure students have real job prospects when their schooling is done.

Sam says when you compare the life that students like Nalwadda can look forward to versus the one she would have had without this help, there is a vast difference. Now Nalwadda has a chance to not just survive, but to thrive.

"[These students] will be the foundation to bring up the community," Sam sums up. "[It's] bringing a ray of hope."

Nalwadda Rose and her large extended family (and possibly a few neighborhood kids).

Rescued

He was just a little kid. Two and a half years old, trudging down the dusty road with a piece of paper in his hand, tears streaming down his cheeks. The director of the orphanage saw him at the edge of the gate.

The boy stretched out his hand, sobbing, not saying a word. The director, Ivan, reached out and took the note. It was from the child's mother, asking the orphanage to take in her son.

Maxim's mother had driven him up the road leading towards the orphanage. The car ride ended with Maxim standing alone on a deserted country lane, abandoned and terrified.

This is the reason Ivan and his church started this orphanage. So many children like Maxim were being abandoned, left for dead, starved, deserted. And no one was doing anything about it.

"You could see many children not being taken care of," Ivan says. "They lived in manholes. They lived underground in sewers."

Some didn't have parents. Some who had parents had sent them to the streets because they had no money to take care of them. Some of the parents were "unfit," Ivan states. The Evangelical Baptist Church in Priazovskoje, Ukraine saw the problem and that no one was doing anything about it.

Something had to be done.

"I shared in the church that we need to pray an institution would be built where we would not just give them food to eat and clothes to wear, but where we would give them spiritual instructions, which is more important," says Ivan, the pastor of the church.

Despite the overwhelming financial obstacles, and with a small congregation of mostly elderly members,

the church opened the Hope Orphanage on property outside of town in 2002.

"We had nothing to start. But our hope was in God and we realized that there was nothing impossible for God. That's why we started to pray about this," Ivan says.

There are now 45 orphans living here; 12 girls and 33 boys. They are cared for, fed, clothed, schooled and taught about the love of Christ.

And kids like Maxim are getting a chance to be normal. A chance to grow and learn and become who they were meant to be.

The power of prayer is not treated lightly within these walls. After all, they've seen it work again and again.

There was the time when the orphanage was about to run out of coal. It was the middle of winter and coal is the building's only source of heat. The man in charge of heating told Ivan he was going to take the last wheelbarrow down to the furnace. And then that would be it.

While he was emptying the last batch, the children

were praying in earnest for a miracle. Before the last piece was used up, Ivan was told that, unbeknownst to them, a man in the United States had wanted to help the orphanage and had decided to buy coal.

"A truck with coal came here and we were asked if we needed some," Ivan recalls. "We Christians know there are no accidents. God showed us His hand that day."

Miracles happen often here. For example, the Ukrainian government has yet to supply financial support to the orphanage, but they have an extensive list of requirements the orphanage must pass to stay in operation.

A team from Canada, under the leadership of Mary, a volunteer from Hungry For Life, visited the orphanage with boxes full of kitchen utensils, cooking implements and other kitchen essentials. The government requirements included having a fully stocked kitchen, and thanks to the Canadian team, the orphanage later passed the inspection.

"We were still in the process of thinking about those things needed for accreditation. But God was already taking care of those things overseas," Ivan said when he found out what the team was bringing to the home.

The orphanage has been getting help from short-term missions teams through the ministry of Pastor John and Nadia Bokoch, Mary's sister. They got involved there more than four years ago, and now each time a team from Canada comes, they go to the orphanage for a visit and to bring assistance in various forms, including financial, moral, spiritual and physical.

There are always challenges here. Money never seems to be enough, government requirements are strict and the old building is always in need of some sort of repair. But through it all, God continues to supply all the needs for the children of the Hope Orphanage in Priazovskoje.

"God is in control of everything," Ivan exclaims. "All glory belongs to God alone."

Boots for Victoria

Victoria needed boots. Winter was coming and she and her siblings had little to wear during the cold Ukrainian winter. Her mother was dying of cancer and the family had no means to care for themselves.

Missionaries John and Nadia heard about the family and began ministering to Victoria, her siblings and her sick mother. As Nadia spent time with the family, she urged them to pray for their needs—big and small.

Victoria took Nadia's advice and began to earnestly pray for God to provide for her family's needs, specifically praying for a pair of boots for herself and a winter coat for her brother. The fervour of her prayers began to worry Nadia, who had great faith but feared those specific prayers might not be answered.

Meanwhile, Nadia's sister, Mary, (who lives in Canada), had gathered clothes to send to Ukraine for distribution. The boxes were already on their way when Nadia heard about the family's clothing needs.

When Mary packed the boxes back in the summer, a woman named Ruthanne heard what she was doing and offered to pack a few boxes and help with the shipping. Ruthanne's family had moved from snowy Winnipeg to the west coast of B.C., so she threw in some winter gear her family didn't need anymore.

The boxes arrived in Ukraine close to Christmas. As Nadia went through the boxes, she found one pair of shoes and one pair of boots. She took them to Victoria and the boots fit perfectly. Victoria had also prayed her brother would have a winter coat. Someone had donated money, which was used to buy her brother a coat.

The family was in awe of God's provision for them in their time of need. Victoria's mother passed away on Christmas Eve that year. Her children tell us she was comforted in knowing God would take care of them after she was gone.

After she died, the kids were going to be sent to separate government orphanages. Nadia fought for the children to stay with their aunt and uncle instead. They already had two children of their own and were living in poverty. But they agreed to take the kids in, at least temporarily.

Victoria's aunt, Oxana, had been skeptical of Victoria's prayers. But when she saw that God provided for these very specific needs, she was surprised and began attending church. She overcame her alcohol addiction and soon after that, became a Christian.

Oxana and her husband decided to permanently take care of her sister's children. While it has been hard financially, Oxana now sees God working in their lives every day.

"There would be circumstances I wouldn't know what to do and I trust God with it and He provides," Oxana says. "Clothing has been provided when needed, there were supplies for my sister when she was really sick. Our family is amazed that people from so far away take care of our needs."

Victoria says other people have also been amazed at how Christians have helped them, how the family has managed to survive, to eat, to have clothing and to become a united family instead of two separate ones living under one roof.

"We are a testimony in our village," Victoria says.

Back in Canada, Ruthanne shares this story of how a simple pair of boots helped open the doors for this family to see Christ's love in action and bring hope to what seemed like a hopeless situation.

"I was the person who sent the boots and shoes," exclaims Ruthanne. "It touched me deeply to realize that God had used the things I gave as a direct answer to someone else's prayers."

Ruthanne (right) sits at her kitchen table in Canada and shares of how a pair of boots was an answer to prayer for Victoria (below).

Siaya Children's Home

The Siaya Children's Home is a place to belong, a place to live protected. But more than that, for the 10 children that live here, it's a place to call home.

We meet the children in the evening inside their modest concrete house. They sing, welcoming us into their presence with songs of worship around a kerosene lamp—the only source of light piercing the dark African night. The children sing with strong voices, accompanied by clapping hands as they move rhythmically to the melody.

Leokadia watches proudly from the side of the room, smiling at her brood. She's the house mother at the orphanage in this small Kenyan community. With a heart for orphans, this Kenyan widow has watched the kids go from hurting, broken, sick children to healthy, thriving and emotionally secure ones.

"All of them had very bad health, now their health is good," Leokadia tells us. Without the home, she adds, "most of them would be dead by now."

The children's histories differ in details but follow a common thread of abandonment, death and tragedy at a young age. Take the case of Margaret. Her parents died when she was young, leaving Margaret to fend for herself. She lived with her grandmother, but "life was difficult," she puts simply.

Margaret's grandmother lives next to the orphanage and is grateful Margaret lives here. She wasn't able to care for Margaret properly, having hardly any food for herself let alone her granddaughter. She knows that here, Margaret will have enough to eat every day and get a good education. Now, she has a chance to succeed.

Then there is Susan. She lost both her parents when she was only seven years old. She was found just wandering in the markets because she had no one to care for her and was brought to the orphanage. She is now a healthy, ambitious teenager who looks after the younger children, does well in school and says when she grows up she would like to become a lawyer.

The children dream big when asked what they would like to achieve with their education. Some would like to grow up to be nurses, others pilots or teachers. One would like to be a preacher, "to spread the word of God," he says.

↖ *The children greet us with songs of worship.*

"They provide us with everything we need," adds Brenda, one of the older girls in the home.

In a letter to Canadian sponsors who made the home a reality, Margaret sums up what the Siaya orphanage means: "Had it not been for you, most of us would be dead by now. We promise to work hard at school so as to be of help to other needy children in the future. We send our love this Christmas and wish you God's blessings in the new year. We all love you. Margaret."

Margaret dances, full of life and full of hope.
↓

The idea of the home is to raise children that will fit into Kenyan culture. They have no electricity, everyone does chores and the kids are learning how to garden—a valuable skill in a subsistence culture. In the home garden, the children grow maize, cow peas, beans, ground nuts, peppers, even watermelon.

When you ask the kids what life is like in the home, you get the answers you'd expect from any normal family. They play together, enjoy singing, share with gusto how good the house mom's cooking is and say she gives them hugs when they're sad and also disciplines them when they're bad.

But when you probe a little deeper, the children begin to reflect on the true value of this home.

"We're being helped," says 12-year-old Steven.

Enoch

Enoch runs and laughs, his black face damp from sweat as he plays in the hot Haitian sun. This is clearly one happy kid, his bright smile visible as he climbs the playground equipment at Haiti Children's Home. It's hard to imagine this child almost didn't make it.

Melinda runs Haiti Children's Home with her mother Patricia Smith, who started the orphanage more than 25 years ago. They often care for premature babies in the orphanage, and have better facilities than the local hospital to care for the early-born infants. They've helped dozens of preemies over the years. One of the ones Melinda will always remember is Enoch.

It was five years ago. A friend of Melinda's was in labour, and she was in trouble. It was nearly three months before the due date, much too early for a hospital with primitive equipment. The hospital staff had already written the baby off, saying there was no way he would be born alive. There was a high risk the mother would die as well. Ever hopeful, Melinda had an incubator waiting at their home and told the hospital she would gladly take the child under her care if he made it through.

Miraculously, both the child and mother survived. They named him Enoch after a Biblical character who lived an exceptionally long and faith-filled life.

Enoch was very tiny and in need of intensive care.

Melinda is a nurse by trade, and did everything she could to help the baby survive. But Enoch didn't respond well to treatment and kept losing weight. When he dropped to one pound and just a few ounces, they stopped weighing him; it was too disheartening.

They ran out of options; all that was left was to pray. He was so fragile, they thought every breath would be his last.

But Melinda had faith.

"The Lord gave me a promise that he would live," she declares.

Melinda heard about a new technique and they decided there was nothing to lose. Called 'Kangaroo care', it's a treatment for premature babies that involves resting the baby on a caregiver's chest, allowing the adult's breathing rhythm to stabilize that of the baby's.

Enoch's father took on this responsibility and would sit still for up to 12 or 13 hours at a time, carefully holding Enoch against his warm chest. His love for his child was overwhelming. And it worked.

Enoch started to eat and slowly gained weight. While still on the mend, Enoch came down with meningitis and two months later was sick again.

Finally, at 13 months, Enoch was healthy and able to go home with his family.

Enoch is now a healthy five-year-old boy, with no mental or physical deformities. It's a source of praise for Enoch's family and for Melinda. From a hospital that gave up on him to a home that wouldn't, Enoch is a living miracle today.

Enoch is now a healthy five-year-old boy.

Southside Church, Chilliwack, B.C.

Southside has been going to Haiti for more than 6 years; they are currently working on a school sponsorship program.

Dump City

It's hard to imagine a world no bigger than the confines of a city dump. Where each day is the same as the last: trudging to a wasteland of refuse, scavenging what little value can be found amidst the trash, and dragging home the day's spoils for a meagre return on a hard day's work in the hot sun.

The dump might sound like an awful place to spend your days and to depend on for your existence. Truthfully, it's worse than awful. It has a stench that makes your stomach turn when you arrive. You can feel the heavy tropical air, surely permeated with toxins, enter your system. With each breath, you know you're breathing in garbage. The smell was so bad, one of our companions promptly threw up as soon as she stepped out of the vehicle.

Mounds of brightly coloured plastic bits, cheap black garbage bags, strips of fabric, styrofoam plates, broken toys and kitchen scraps covered in flies create the work space for these citizens. Dust blankets the air as torrents of refuse pours out the backside of garbage trucks. But instead of backing away, the poverty-stricken gather as closely as they can to the stream of trash to try and grab the most valuable recyclables first.

Adding to the eery, surreal sight are the vultures. They swoop in and scan the garbage, picking through it with their razor-sharp beaks, menacing black wings flapping as they prowl. They look just as ready to bite your eye sockets as eat the garbage.

This isn't a new phenomenon in Manta, Ecuador. Families have worked here for generations, with children following in the same footsteps as their parents and grandparents—a sad legacy. It is a place seemingly without hope. But a small and dedicated group of Christians are working to change this reality.

When the Por Amor Foundation began ministering in this area, children also spent their days working here. They would stand under the trucks as they dumped the waste to help find recyclables. We're told a child died doing this and that's why they're now banned. We met a man working here named Carlos. He has one daughter who used to work at the dump but who now attends school. It didn't seem unusual to Carlos to have a small child working in such hazardous conditions. After all, he's been toiling here since he was just a little kid more than 25 years ago.

When asked how he manages to endure the hard labour day in and day out, Carlos states simply, "I don't have any other livelihood."

Por Amor wants to help break this cycle of poverty by ensuring the children of these scavengers are educated. As of three years ago, children were banned from working at the dump. Por Amor helps by providing students with a backpack and basic supplies at the start of the school year and promoting education in the community. They've also brought in a summer vacation Bible school for the kids.

Por Amor helps in other practical ways as well, such as providing adult education, giving them the courage and confidence to move from this life of subsistence. The organization hosts a Christmas party every year, giving out gift baskets of food staples and a chicken.

Anything they can do within their limited resources, Por Amor does for these dump city residents.

Por Amor's aid reaches more than 150 of the poorest families that scratch out a living in this dismal place. The organization has brought hope to many, including a woman named Jesús.

She has been here for more years than she can count—a permanent fixture in an ever-shifting landscape. Jesús cares for her sick daughter and her niece who has deformed feet.

"I do this to work and help my family," Jesús says as she pauses from the hot and exhausting labour. Yet Jesús toils with a smile, a look of contentment resting on her face. Her demeanour stands in stark contrast to the reality around her, and we inquire about her obvious joy. It turns out, Jesús became a Christian when a short-term missions team with Por Amor led an evangelism meeting right at the dump. She is happy because she accepted Christ into her life and found a joy that wasn't there before.

While the world goes on, oblivious to this marginalized population, Por Amor brings hope to a people in the greatest need of love and a helping hand. And that takes courage; this is not a nice place. Before we leave, we give one last look around the scene: men and women who look older than they should, slowly and methodically picking and tearing and searching. Vultures swoop and scream.

We gladly return to the jeep, lather hand sanitizer on our skin and peel dusty bandanas off our faces. As we drive away from this awful place we can see Jesús at work again, hunched over heaps of garbage. The visitors provided a brief distraction, now it's back to the reality she and the others live every day. With one hand in a dirty, old rubber glove and one hand holding a sack, Jesús picks through the refuse, a smile on her face.

Jesús has been here for more years than she can count. →

With each breath, you know you're breathing in garbage.

Leiton's smile

It was his grin that caught my attention. Leiton stood out from the many kids streaming from the school bus and down the dirt steps leading to the Montanita Verde Children's Home in San Lorenzo, Ecuador. He smiled from ear to ear like he had a big secret to share; you could tell this kid loved life. He spotted a new face and came ripping towards me, halted at my feet and promptly showed me how he could undo and do up his blue school uniform tie.

I couldn't speak Spanish, he couldn't speak English. It didn't really seem to matter though to Leiton, he was just proud to show someone his skill.

At lunchtime, Leiton made every effort he could to talk to me. I finally figured out he was asking where I was from. When I replied, "Canada," that trademark Leiton grin beamed even brighter. He'd heard of this country, and was obviously pleased to meet someone from so far away. He jabbered away over lunch, figuring I'd catch on I suppose.

I got a chance to talk to Leiton with the help of a translator, and that grin did not leave his face through the whole interview. I asked him why he smiles.

"Because of the family I have here," he replied.

The director of the orphanage tells us that 8-year-old Leiton and his 18-month-old brother, Justin, arrived at the orphanage just two months before we came.

You'd never guess the backstory of this seemingly happy child.

Leiton and Justin's mother works as a prostitute. She drinks, even through pregnancy. She's had numerous abortions. When they came to the orphanage, Justin didn't have a birth certificate and Leiton had never gone to school. There were obvious signs of neglect with both children. Other family members are not much better than their mother; the social system in Ecuador has decided the best people to take care of these two young children are complete strangers instead of anyone from their own family.

Leiton and Justin were the first kids to come to this family-style home set up at the orphanage. House parents Pepe and Karen tell us that when they first arrived, Justin had physical problems—he had cysts on his face from bites that hadn't been cleaned properly. Leiton had emotional problems—he would start crying and hit his head repeatedly against a wall when disciplined.

Pepe and Karen put Leiton into school and a tutor now works with him to help transition into the world of education. At eight years of age, Leiton is just now learning to write his alphabet, and could proudly spell his name for me. Karen says he's learning to take discipline well, and is listening and responding instead of physically hurting himself.

Meanwhile, Justin has really connected to Pepe and Karen like parents. He cries when Pepe goes to work and excitedly runs to him when he comes home. The boys are learning to trust and accept love in a safe and secure home.

In only two months, the director and the house parents agree they have seen dramatic change in Leiton and Justin. Most importantly, the brothers have found a loving home here at Montanita Verde.

A school teacher's heart

Sandra looks up to the rafters in her simple room and then down to her hands, her shoulders shaking with unabated sobs.

Sandra is the lone school teacher at a simple, wood-frame boarding school in the heart of the Copper Canyon. It's a place so insignificant to the world, it doesn't even show up on a map. A single mattress on a wooden platform and a rough-hewn desk are all the furniture in her sparse accommodations, where she sits and shares her story.

Sandra, a 24-year-old Mexican from the bustling city of Juarez, is a long way from home. She's here to help the children of the Canyon, the Tarahumara Indians.

She first heard the call to missions 10 years ago when her pastor shared his vision to build a school for the neglected children of the Copper Canyon. Sandra felt God prompting her to be a part of this ministry as its teacher. As an orphan herself, she identified with the children. When the school opened in Guacaivo last year, there was Sandra with open arms, ready for the kids who had to be taught how to hug.

Tarahumara live completely outside of the 21st century. Many still live in caves, sleeping in craggy rock outcroppings inside the canyon walls. Before this school was built in the middle of Tarahumara territory, most of the children had never gone to school. The ones that did go had to trek a long and treacherous canyon route, on a path that took us five hours to hike—one way.

They came because of the promise of three square meals a day. They stayed because of the love Sandra showed them and the promise of a better life for their future. There are 40 children living under Sandra's care. During the school year they are fed, taught about God's love and given an education.

Sandra's heart has been broken for these kids. She cries because she knows the desperate situations they come from and what they must return to when the school year ends. She cries for the lost people living in the tiny settlements carved onto the steep mountainsides. She has seen the desperate circumstances they come from, and prays their future is brighter than their past.

With God's love in her heart, Sandra has reached into the lives of these unreached children and shown them Jesus.

Sandra surrounded by a sea of her kids.

Learning to hug

Teachers usually teach the ABC's. What Sandra wasn't expecting was the need to teach her students the word 'love' and how to hug.

"When the kids come in, it's like they're coming to another world," Sandra describes.

Children are not cherished in Tarahumara culture, and Sandra describes their treatment like that of slaves. Young children are forced to work in the fields by relatives who care little for their well-being. Some of the children are orphans. Others have parents, but they are unable or unwilling to take care of their kids.

The opportunity for an education was unheard of for most of these children before now. And Sandra sees the boarding school giving the students and the Tarahumara people a chance to survive.

"Education is important to better their future. If the kids learn to read and write, they will know what they are, they'll know their rights," Sandra says. "They will be the change of the whole nation."

In the short time the school has been open, there has already been change in the children. Sandra shares that sometimes if it has been a long day, she will tell the children just to go to sleep. They insist they cannot go to bed until they have done their prayer time.

"I see how they give their hearts to the Lord," she says. "This is a wonderful place to invest because we're going to have a great harvest."

Brenda

Brenda was no stranger to travel when her church in Kitimat, B.C. got involved in global missions. In fact, she and her husband have been all over the world, lending a hand on short-term trips.

So when Mountainview Alliance Church partnered with Pastor Tomas and his ministry that works with natives in remote Mexican villages, Brenda was quick to sign up.

"To do short-term missions—that's so my heart," says Brenda. "I love to go and rub shoulders with the people, especially Christians in another country and another culture."

The team traveled to Babicora, a small village of Pima Indians located on the summit of Mexico's grand Copper Canyon. The Pima mistrust outsiders and were against Pastor Tomas even talking about God when he first met them. Slowly, through building relationships and gaining trust, Pastor Tomas has seen barriers starting to come down in this community.

While in Babicora, Brenda met a couple named Cristobal and Elena. Cristobal had become friends with another team member, Kevin, during the church's first trip. Brenda grew close to Cristobal's wife, and together she and Kevin would walk to this couple's home to have coffee and get to know one another.

"The more I went to their home, the more I fell in love with the family," she says.

Two days before they left, Brenda and Kevin once again visited Cristobal and Elena. As they headed back, Brenda turned around and saw them still standing by their home, staring at their departing guests.

"My heart broke," Brenda shares. "I thought, 'In two days we get to leave and we're going back to our comfortable little Canada and you guys are still here'. I just cried and cried. That's one of those God-moments, where God really captured my heart."

She knows God was telling her at that moment that missions is about more than just going to see the world. It's about relationships.

Brenda's home is filled with keepsakes from her world travels. But one of her most precious mementos is a small jar of canned peaches. Elena gave it to her, a token of her friendship and appreciation.

"Their gift was so small. We had given them a bag of clothes and food and all this kind of stuff. But she sacrificed to give something to me," says

"Here I am, honoured, that out of her poverty she gave this."

Brenda. "Here I am, honoured, that out of her poverty she gave this."

The jar sits in Brenda's kitchen as a reminder to pray for Elena. And it reminds her that missions is about more than just travel and having a cultural experience. She's blown away by the connections made with people from such a different world, and her relationships built in Babicora have led Brenda to return to Mexico again and again.

"It's like you share heartstrings with them—and it's the same with the people on the team—it's just a whole amazing atmosphere of 'we're one in this'. And even though you can't speak the same language, you share the same heart and the same God and the same Jesus who loves us."

Brenda with Cristobal, Elena and their children.

Remember Seje

In Kenya, in the middle of nowhere, lies a village of great value. You wouldn't think it from looking around, but this community holds worth. Just not in the eyes of the world.

In the world's eyes, Seje means nothing. There are no capital assets here. There are no resources to draw from the land. There's no economy, hence no economic growth. There is no quality in the soil for growing crops. There is no water, no rain and no hope.

But there is value found in Seje: the people.

Men. Women. Families. Broken families, devastated by poverty. There's children. And there are two teachers who care enough to want a better life for these kids.

Seje is little more than an array of huts about five kilometres from the nearest village, which at least has a corner store.

The only way to find the school is to follow a long thin ribbon of red dirt that someone had the sense of humour to call a road. It bumps and winds and has potholes so big I was concerned we would be abandoning the car and walking with our field partner, Edgar, to find it.

We arrived to our destination—a dusty patch of land with two buildings. Inside the mud walls of the first room, children welcome their rare visitors from outside the community. Sunlight streams into the windows, the only source of light.

The Seje school, with somewhere between 90 and 160 students depending on the day, can hardly be described as a school. While it has some of the building blocks of a school—desks and a chalkboard notably—there is little else to distinguish these two mud buildings as a place of learning.

For starters, there are very few books. In fact, the grade 3 class has no books for their level. There is only one master book for grade 3 and that book is on-loan from another school.

The teachers have no pens to write with and to grade the students' work. Not that it matters much of the time; most of the children don't have an exercise book. Exercise books cost mere pennies but even that is too much money for families. Unlike most Kenyan schools, only some of the kids here wear uniforms. The red and white outfits are tattered and threadbare.

The supply room has empty bottles of medicine. If children are injured at school, there is literally nothing Peter and Lillian can do for them. No antiseptics, no cleansers, not even a bandaid.

Even the flagpole, which once helped to distinguish the school as something legitimate, has been eaten by termites. The flag now sits folded inside a cupboard, next to the room where older local boys camp at night with a spear to protect what little material goods the school has from thieves.

Most of the students are orphans, living wherever they

can find a sympathetic hand or with old grandparents in need of assistance themselves.

While the story of the children is sad, it was listening to the teachers share that really broke my heart. Lillian and Peter teach kindergarten to grade 4, alternating classrooms for different subjects.

Lillian is from Seje and has three of her own children. Peter, who has five children, bikes to work each day from a community called Siaya, more than 15 kilometres away.

The two teachers work very hard, sacrificing more than you could imagine to give these young kids a chance at a future.

Since the school is not registered, it gets no assistance from the government. That means Lillian and Peter are volunteers and receive no salary from the Kenyan government. The school needs major construction in order for the government to register it. Yet the government won't supply the funding for construction because the school is not registered as official. And there is no hope of the community banding together for funding. There is no work in Seje. There is no rain for the farmers. And there is no opportunity for the citizens here to ever get out of their own poverty enough to help others.

Yet every Monday through Friday, Lillian and Peter come to school ready to teach. Why, I ask, do they not go and work somewhere and make a living? Lillian answers that if they do not teach these kids, no one will. And they can't give up on them or there will be no future for the kids of Seje.

"It's a call from God," says Lillian. "If I leave, then God cannot be happy with me. I want to give them something, to show them education is important."

They live on faith that God will provide a way for the school to continue.

There was hope for this village once. A church signed on to help. A feeding program was started for the school kids. Money was sent for salaries, for school

For teachers Peter & Lillian, it's more than just a job.

supplies, for medicine. A water tank was installed so when it rained there would be water.

But as things sometimes go, it didn't work out and the church stopped supporting the school. The feeding program ended, the money stopped coming. The water tank sits as a cruel reminder as there is no rain and hasn't been for a long time.

I ask Lillian where she gets her water for drinking.

"There is none," she replies. "I just go thirsty."

With no money, Lillian cannot even feed her children and herself save for the kindness of others. She is sometimes so weak, she can barely stand in front of the class and teach.

"These children need somebody standing, running with them," Lillian says. She worries that if she gives up on these kids, they will never see education as something important and will be trapped in Seje by the same poverty that has haunted generations before them.

As I sit on a comfy bed having just eaten a deliciously filling dinner, I think of Peter and Lillian probably going to bed hungry tonight. I think of Peter biking the long and extremely difficult road to school. I think of Lillian hearing her children moan from the hunger pangs. I think of the random student who surely will hurt herself playing in the dirt and the teachers having nothing to give her for the pain. I think of the cruel joke played on the school, with a large water tank sitting in the middle of the yard and not a drop of water in sight. And I think of how much just a little money would help these people.

Peter said something during our interview that stuck with me. He spoke about a verse in Proverbs that reads if a man wants to eat, he must work. Then he laughed at the irony.

"We work and still don't eat," he says wryly.

Yet by staying, Peter and Lillian demonstrate that these kids matter. They show by their actions that Seje holds value and is worth fighting for.

Since the writing of this story, Hillside Community Church in Coquitlam, B.C. has pledged to help the community of Seje. With Hillside's involvement, Seje now has five classrooms, a water tank rain retention system, a new sports field and supplies. They are also seeking ways to fund a water well. More importantly, Hillside has brought hope back to Seje.

"I want to have a greater part in helping eradicate poverty.

Poverty is real and devastating...but God's power is greater and through faith and action those who suffer can know hope and freedom."

—Jenny, Hillside Church, Coquitlam, B.C.

Eriberto

Eriberto walked for hours just to share his story. We don't know how long it took him; time is not really a relevant detail to the highland Quechua people of Peru. Neither is distance. What is important is community.

Community means everything here. Families grow up in the same village generation after generation. Children tend to the flocks their parents raised. For many, their village is where they are born, live their whole lives, and die without ever setting foot in the modern city of Cusco.

Standing on a rough grassy field by the elementary school in a tiny mountain village, Eriberto wears a Stetson-style black hat with a strip of brown leather stretched around the band. His blue checkered shirt is buttoned up neatly underneath his bright red jacket. It's fairly cool in the morning at 11,000 feet, surrounded on all sides by green mountains.

Eriberto was a leader at his church in Corribumba and was responsible for the care of nine other churches in surrounding communities. Often in these churches it becomes a case of the blind leading the blind as many Christians can't read the Bible and most have no qualified pastor to lead. About six years ago, Eriberto and other church leaders gathered together to discuss their fledgling churches. They knew they needed training to effectively lead their congregations. However, they weren't sure how to accomplish this task. None of the leaders had ever had formal education and financially they couldn't afford to go to school. It was "impossible," Eriberto shares.

That's when Eriberto heard about ATEK, a Christian organization that works with Cusco-Quechua communities to train leaders—leaders who can teach, who can preach, who can minister to husbands and wives and children. It's training that is simply not accessible to these remote communities otherwise.

Today in Eriberto's village, ATEK-trained teachers are now leading marriage counselling, literacy training and alcohol education, as well as pastoral discipleship. He has seen his church strengthened where before it seemed ready to die. The faith of the Christians in Corribumba grew, and he says they're now aware of their responsibilities as Christians.

But even more encouraging than the spiritual growth in the church has been the change Eriberto has seen in his own life. He and his wife took ATEK's marriage counselling. The sessions opened his eyes to what a marriage could be, such as praying together and making decisions as a couple.

"Even though I was a minister and was teaching and baptizing, I never fully understood that marriage is a covenant," he reflects.

"It's a blessing from God. ATEK is like a medicine for the problems in our villages."

Now Eriberto and his wife are happy in their marriage, and they travel to villages far and near to lead marriage counselling sessions.
Eriberto says without ATEK, Corribumba and the other communities would still be full of spiritual sickness and misunderstanding.

"It's a blessing from God. ATEK is like a medicine for the problems in our villages," he concludes.

Eriberto walked for hours to share his story with us.

159

Beach Corner

The people at Beach Corner Evangelical Free Church knew God had called them to short-term missions. They had a vision to go and serve. The problem was where they should go.

The church, located in the small prairie town of Stony Plain, Alberta, had done missions work in Mexico. But the work wasn't productive and it left the church wanting more.

They wanted a missions focus where they could actually make and see a difference. Through Hungry For Life, Beach Corner connected with a ministry in Peru called ATEK. The first trip affirmed this was where Beach Corner was supposed to be.

"It unified the vision way better than expected," says Pastor Bill. "There was a connection made between our church and ATEK."

The people in the villages were in awe that Christians would come from so far away to see them and many gained a new understanding of what it means to be a follower of Christ.

"One guy said 'Before you came, I thought Christianity was for the poor people and the illiterate'," shares Pastor Bill. "We found just our presence made a difference. And when you show that you love people, they respond."

Beach Corner now sends one to two missions teams a year to work with ATEK, an organization that ministers to the native Cusco-Quechua people of Peru. While Beach Corner's assistance to ATEK has been invaluable, back in Stony Plain it's apparent it has helped on the home front as well. The focus on missions has empowered and unified the church body, and has strengthened the faith of those who have gone to Peru.

For Taylor, who was 17 when he went, it was an experience that allowed him to see how the poor can be so rich in faith, and to see how blessed he is to live in North America.

"It sounds so cliché about a missions trip, but it really did change me," Taylor says. "God worked in amazing ways."

The church leadership would like to see every church attendee involved in some way or another with the Peru missions. That's how Mike Stobbe ended up on one of the first trips. As a Board member, he knew it was important to travel to see first-hand what impact the church was having.

"It was where God wanted me to be," Mike recalls.

He's glad he got a chance to see the impact in Peru, but he's also glad to see the impact missions has had on his church.

"A lot of people have said that the Spirit is working in our church. People come to our church and say it feels like home," Mike says.

Pastor Bill has seen the blessing God has poured on Beach Corner since their commitment to Peru began, and is glad to be a part of something that is helping so many people—both in Canada and Peru.

"When you seek to follow the vision God gives you, He honours that," says Pastor Bill.

Slums and the 'so what'

Slum |sləm|

noun.

– a squalid and overcrowded urban street or district inhabited by very poor people.

– a house or building unfit for human habitation.

The slums of Moratuwa, Sri Lanka, certainly fit this description. This is not an area fit for human habitation, though thousands of men, women and children do. It is squalid. It is overcrowded. It is ignored.

It is not a pretty place.

Dirt pathways are swept by fervent moms as their children play amongst the small shanties nestled row on row. Garbage is piled on the beach, next to the lone communal tap. There is a quiet desperation yet an obvious pride found in the people here. They might not have much, but it's a place to call home.

So what? You know there are poor people in the world. You know there are slums and poverty and people who need love and care. Why do you need to hear more?

For me, I need to share these stories because we can't ignore it anymore. We've seen and met people whose entire lives could be transformed for a few dollars a day. People who would love their kids to have a chance at life, a chance to grow and become who they were meant to be. We've met them, we've sat in their homes on the best chairs available, which are often seats we'd find relegated to the trash pile. We've seen the desperation and the fear.

But that's why we care. Why should you?

I think it's because God cares. He cares for the sea of unknown and forgotten, the poor and destitute. The Lord cares for these people. These unknown people on the other side of the world. And He knows each and every one of them by name.

He knows people like Sujani Priyangika. She and her husband, Upul Hemantha, live in a partition of her mother's shanty. They had a home, but it was swept away in a horrible tsunami in December 2004. They are raising their daughter, Tharushika, on not much more than love. Sujani and Upul take turns selling lottery tickets in a street-side stall, which makes little money at the best of times.

Tharushika goes to a day program—an early learning education centre—run by Christians living in Moratuwa. They are showing God's love and care to the residents of this slum. They believe that each person matters, and they're trying to help families by providing education to kids like Tharushika. The Beach Children's Centre cannot do much, but for 23 children attending the daily program, it's a better start than they ever would have had otherwise.

Mothers like Sujani are hoping their children's education will be their whole family's ticket out of here. That is, if they're not physically kicked out of the slum first. This meagre patch of earth the impoverished have carved out for a home is being threatened. Tharushkina's parents and hundreds of neighbours have been labelled squatters and given notice to leave, Sunjani says. And according to Sunjani, the government has not offered anywhere else for the poorest of the poor to go. And so they stay.

"We will have nowhere to go. The government gave the date to get out, but nobody left," Sujani tells us through a translator. "One day the police will come and kick us out…" she trails off and looks outside, through the broken wire mesh window.

The Bible tells us to hear the cries of the poor and needy, and defend their cause. I have no way of keeping in touch with Sujani, and it certainly won't make international news if this slum is ever cleared out by police. But my brief encounter with one family living in this impoverished land has stuck in my brain.

Tharushika, Sujani, and Upul are just one family, living thousands of miles away from me on a small island nation. According to the United Nations, there are 1.4 billion people living in extreme poverty conditions. I know that even if I had a good salary, I couldn't help all the people we met, people like Sujani, let alone a fraction of the more than one billion people facing serious starvation conditions.

As I've reflected on the scores of people we met who are poor and hungry, widowed or orphaned, alone and in need of support, I've struggled with what to do. So what does God ask of me? What does He ask of you?

> *"Defend the cause of the weak and fatherless; maintain the rights of the poor and oppressed."*
> PSALM 82:3

And if we don't obey, then we don't even know the Lord…

> *"'He defended the cause of the poor and needy, and so all went well. Is that not what it means to know me?' declares the LORD."* JEREMIAH 22:16

Or He won't listen to our own prayers…

> *"If a man shuts his ears to the cry of the poor, he too will cry out and not be answered."* PROVERBS 21:13

And the Lord gives us promises that our efforts will be well worth it…

> *"Sell your possessions and give to the poor. Provide purses for yourselves that will not wear out, a treasure in heaven that will not be exhausted, where no thief comes near and no moth destroys. For where your treasure is, there your heart will be also."*
> LUKE 12:33–34

I think all of this means that while I can't help everyone who's poor, I do need to do my part. I need to spend myself on behalf of the poor and oppressed. I can't wait and pray for God to give me a six-figure salary so I can be generous. Maybe you feel called to help Tharushika. Maybe your heart goes out to Ugandan orphans or to Ukrainian widows or to the lonely living in your local care home. Whatever it is, I think God is calling each one of us to do what we can.

In some ways, I've had a hard time dealing with the aftermath of travel, with the 'so what' that comes when you see enormous poverty and then come back home to enormous wealth and waste. And processing stories like Tharushika's and verses like the ones listed above is something I have been working through and something I needed to share. I would encourage you to pray and ask God where He would have you fulfill His clear instructions in the Bible. Where should your time, your money, your talents be directed?

Seek the Lord, listen to His calling and obey.

My brief
encounter
with one family
living in this
impoverished
land has stuck
in my brain.

Our story

It started with a walk. After church one Sunday, we decided to meander the paths of a local park in Chilliwack, B.C.

We had just sold our apartment in an unsteady real estate market and actually made a profit. We got to talking about what we could do with the money: buy a nice house or renovate a fixer-upper, maybe do some travel or invest in savings. But as we talked about it, we realized the windfall was God's blessing and it should be used for His glory, not our own.

Justin is a graphic designer and an avid photographer with a keen eye for the perfect shot. I'm a journalist by trade, covering the goings-on of life in small-town B.C. We went to talk to Dave Blundell at Hungry For Life (HFL), which is based in Chilliwack, to see if he knew of any Christian organizations that could use our skills for a project. He said HFL would love to work with us to create something to illustrate what God is doing around the world.

Neither of us had ever pictured ourselves getting involved in missions and we certainly weren't qualified for such a task.

Neither of us had ever pictured ourselves getting involved in missions and we certainly weren't qualified for such a task. But we felt God was calling us to this opportunity just as HFL was seeking a way to share stories about how short-term teams and project partners were impacting lives, both at home and overseas.

And so Pockets of Change was born, a vague idea that turned into a concept that turned into a mission statement: "By using specific stories of the spiritual and physical transformation of people and communities, we desire to motivate individuals to be a part of a movement of compassion and justice, realizing their potential to effect global change."

Partnered with HFL, we visited over a dozen different projects in developing nations across the globe. We flew 78,200 kilometres on 27 flights, slept in 50 different beds and travelled to 10 countries. Along the way, we collected 26,796 photos and 252 interviews. Everyone we met had a story to tell. And along the way, we found our own story too.

When we started Pockets of Change, we had been married nine years. We'd never planned to have children and were happy with our dual-income, no-kids lifestyle. But as we traveled, God began to transform our hearts. Poverty-stricken people in dire

circumstances felt sorry for us when they found out we were childless. One example stands out: while in Ukraine, we met with a severely disabled woman who was abandoned by her husband and was raising her son and daughter alone. Through a translator, she asked if we had any children. When we said no, I could see her face drop with sadness for us. I had felt sorry for her, yet she pitied me.

By the time we were back in Canada working on the book, we knew without a doubt we wanted children. Within two months, we were pregnant. We've never been more thankful for anything in our lives than when we became parents. God has blessed us with two beautiful children. We can guarantee that if it weren't for us stepping out in faith when God called us to this project, we would not be parents today.

We hope that by reading this book, you are encouraged in your own faith. We hope you can see the good being done in this world through organizations like HFL, their partners around the world and especially through individuals willing to step out of their comfort zones, travel to a foreign land and serve in whatever way God asks. We hope you realize that you too, can see your potential to effect global change simply by saying 'yes' to what God is asking of you.

So what's your story?

Index

CPSIA information can be obtained
at www.ICGtesting.com
Printed in the USA
LVIW020917060513
332252LV00001B

9780991769605

Hungry For Life
INTERNATIONAL

45950 Alexander Avenue
Chilliwack, BC V2P 1L5
Phone: 1-604-703-0223

138 E. 12300 S. Suite C-222
Draper, Utah 84020
Phone: 1-801-979-6453

www.hungryforlife.org

ADDITIONAL PHOTO CREDITS

Ryan Toyota, iii, 117
Lorene Keitch, 5, 168–169
Kelly Edgeley, 10–11, 160–161
Ben Zimmer, 10–11
HFL, 85, 151
Brian Clarkson, 100–101
Coquitlam Alliance Church, 111
Steve Dove, 141
Ginnie Frede, 168